BETWEEN 2 WORLDS

How to Win the Battle Between
Two Worlds That Challenge You Daily

WRITTEN BY
ELIZABETH WALCOTT
EVANGELIST AND PROPHET OF GOD

Copyright © 2025 by Elizabeth Walcott
Between Two Worlds

ISBN: 978-1-938443-46-0
All rights reserved.

No portion of this book may be reproduced in any form without written permission from the publisher or author, except as permitted by U.S. copyright law.

Disclaimer JDN Publications/EDUCATE Publishing is a self-publishing platform that offers authors the opportunity to publish their works without going through an editorial selection process. The authors are responsible for the content of their works, and in particular, JDN/EDUCATE does not necessarily agree with the content of this book. We are not responsible for errors in it, and we do not assume any responsibility for the consequences of reading it. Readers should be aware that the content of this book is the sole responsibility of the author. Printed in the United States of America

CONTENT

Dedication..5

Introduction...6

Chapter 1: The War Between Two World.............................16

Chapter 2: Entering the Spirit World Through Portals.........20

Chapter 3: Jehovah Will Be With His People........................26

Chapter 4: Oath of Allegiance..30

Chapter 5: The Power of His Name.......................................42

Chapter 6: Christ, Change Your Name..................................56

Chapter 7: The Price..64

Chapter 8: Two Worlds, Open Your Eyes!............................72

Chapter 9: We Are Commanding Generals...........................78

Chapter 10: I'm A Tool In My Father's Hands......................82

Chapter 11: When the Devil Takes Away What You Love Most............94

Chapter 12: Jehovah's Kingdom Vs. Satan's.......................100

Chapter 13: Father...112

Chapter 14: Regional Intercession.......................................120

Chapter 15: Knowing Your Enemies....................................134

Chapter 16: Other Areas of Attack.......................................146

Chapter 17: Men Prepared For Spiritual Warfare...............158

Chapter 18: You Are A Weapon of War...............................168

About The Author..186

References..187

DEDICATION

First, I thank my Heavenly Father, my children, and all who supported me and believe in my ministry. That is why I dedicate this book to the Father first and then to all those who helped me grow, my beloved and friend, prophetess Virginia, who taught me the first steps of what it means to be a prophet of God. Pastor Virginia never imagines why I love her so much. In my early years of ministry, I remember hearing her speak on behalf of God, with a voice of authority. I always wondered how she did it, and I said to God, "How beautiful it is to hear God speak through this prophet, Virginia." Until one day, God took me in the spirit through one of the services of my spiritual mother, pastor Teresa. My pastor, Teresa, never stood between God and what God wanted to speak to the people. From that day on, my life changed. I felt part of the office of prophets; she is like a spiritual mother, similar to when prophets meet and speak the same language or language in the Old Testament.

INTRODUCTION

Take Ownership of What's Yours

Between Two Worlds became real to me, both physically and spiritually. While I was stationed in Germany for three years, one day the Lord put this word in my heart: "Between Two Worlds." At the moment, I didn't understand anything, but then in the army, I was assigned to a new place called Rock Island. When I came to the United States, I saw the place where the base is physically, it is located between two states, Iowa and Illinois, I am literally between two places, which are only separated by a "bridge." There, I was able to understand what the Lord showed me, that He sent me to this place for a purpose. God strategically placed me in that region.

In this place, God has blessed me, and now I have a Pastor who is in the same apostolic and prophetic office, Pastor Reece of River City Church in Moline, Illinois. A place where I have been congregating, in addition to attending Pastor Harrigan's Church in Kansas City. God strategically sent me there because he is lining up his people in strategic places so that he can tear down the walls of the devil and his kingdom and continue to establish the Kingdom of Christ, taking territories and nations for Him through the Holy Spirit.

The spiritual realm is just as real as the physical realm; the two fight each other, but only one child of God dares to enter the spiritual world with all the armor that Christ has given us as his children. It has not been easy to enter and stay in this region, I have had stronger wars in this place; but I have seen the hand of God moving as never before; where I see the more I see the hosts of wickedness in the spirit, the more I see the power of God at work in the atmosphere; only the brave dare to take possession of what God has given them in certain territorial places, the more the enemy attacks the more I have seen the Glory of God and his purpose fulfilled.

10 So Saul tried to nail David with his spear to the wall, but he turned away from Saul's presence, and he struck the wall with his spear. and David fled, and escaped that night. 11 Then Saul sent messengers to David's house to watch him, and kill him in the morning. But Michal his wife told David, saying, "If you do not save your life tonight, tomorrow you will be killed." 12 And Michal took David down through a window; and he went away and fled, and escaped. 13 Then Michal took a statue and laid it on the bed, and put a pillow of goat's hair on the headboard and covered it with his clothes. 14 And when Saul sent messengers to arrest David, she answered, "He is sick." 15 Saul sent messengers again to see David, saying, "Bring me to bed so that I may kill him." 16 And when the messengers came in, behold, the image was on the bed, and a pillow of goat's hair at its head. 17 Then Saul said to Michal, "Why have you deceived me like this, and let my enemy escape? And Michal said to Saul, "For he said to me, Let me go; if not, I will kill you. 18 So David fled and escaped, and came to Samuel at Ramah, and told him all that Saul had done with him. And he and Samuel went and dwelt in Naioth. 19 And word was given to Saul, saying, Behold, David is at Naioth in Ramah. 20 Then Saul sent messengers to bring David, and they saw a company of prophets prophesying, and Samuel standing there and presiding over them. And the Spirit of God came upon Saul's messengers, and they also prophesied. 21 When Saul heard about it, he sent other messengers, who also prophesied. And Saul sent messengers a third time, and they also prophesied. 22 Then he himself went to Ramah; And when he came to the great well that is in Sheku, he asked, "Where are Samuel and David?" And one answered, "Behold, they are in Naioth in Ramah." 23 And he went to Naioth in Ramah; and the Spirit of God also came upon him, and he kept walking and prophesying until he came to Naioth in Ramah. 24 And he also stripped off his garments, and prophesied likewise before Samuel, and was naked all that day and all that night. Hence it was said, "Saul also among the prophets?" (1 Samuel 19:10-24 KJV).

Saul represents someone envious, jealous, someone whom God has rejected, and has been replaced by someone whom God chose. Look at what he says in verse 15,

"Saul again sent messengers to see David, saying,

'Bring me to bed that I may kill him."

Saul was persistent, and so was the enemy. Just because you achieve victory in a situation doesn't mean the enemy will surrender. Demons are organized; they can attack at any time, whether you are spiritually weak or strong. In this context, David sought out the prophet Samuel, the one who had anointed both Saul and David. David and Samuel traveled to Naioth in Ramah, where Samuel lived. Elkanah, Samuel's father, was familiar with this place. Ramah had an altar to Jehovah, and the elders of Israel knew where it was located. It is puzzling to consider how a king like Saul was unaware of Ramah's significance.

David was anointed there, which suggests that Saul showed little interest in meeting prophets, especially Samuel, who had anointed him. Instead of being consumed by jealousy and attempting to eliminate those whom God had chosen in his stead, Saul should have focused on his duties as king. How did David know where to find the prophet? Men who genuinely seek to hear God's voice tend to unite with those in prophetic ministries, unafraid of what God may reveal. This is why I believe David sought refuge in the holy place where the prophet resided; the pure in heart will often be shunned by those with corrupt intentions.

If you seek a place of refuge, consider Ramah, where the atmosphere is conducive to hearing the voice of the Father. Moses also needed assistance from the prophets, calling upon 70 men who were filled with the Spirit of Moses, which represents the Holy Spirit.

> *"17 And I will go down and speak with you there, and I will take of the spirit that is in you, and I will put in them; and they shall bear with thee the burden of the people, and thou shalt not bear it alone" (Numbers 11:17).*

Many individuals involved in ministry often hesitate to receive prophecies from others, believing that God speaks directly to them. The seventy men mentioned were filled with the Holy Spirit that Jehovah bestowed upon Moses to assist him in his ministry, enabling him to lead the people into the Promised Land.

> *25 Then the LORD came down in the cloud and spoke to him; and he took of the spirit that was in him, and put it in the seventy old men; and when the Spirit rested upon them, they prophesied, and did not cease" (Numbers 11:25).*

Both Saul and his men experienced something profound; just as the 70 men who assisted Moses were filled with the Holy Spirit—some to minister and aid Moses, and others to witness God's power. In David's case, when one persecutes an anointed person, staying close to that individual allows them to receive some of the anointing. Samuel was among the prophets, and when Saul's men arrived, they were prophesying. Although the Bible does not detail their spiritual lives, it is evident that they were witnesses of God's power.

Saul was left powerless; all his authority as king was stripped away. When you find yourself in the right place, those who seek your downfall will be overwhelmed by God's glory and will not be able to deny that the Lord is with you. This underscores the importance of being filled with God's presence and surrounding yourself with people of similar gifts, so those gifts can work in harmony for the church's growth. A pastor, evangelist, or teacher does not shy away from prophecy or the voice of God; they abandon the excuse that most prophets are false, recognizing that many have been chosen by the Lord for this time.

A person full of resentment and hatred desires to see you fail, just as Saul sent men to kill David, paralleling how the enemy sought to destroy everything about Job. Saul literally aimed to kill the anointed one; the enemy will attack anyone who follows God's will. However, after David played the harp, the evil spirit tormenting Saul departed, bringing him peace.

How is it possible to help those who wish to harm you? People who malign others, saying, *"Bring me to him so I can destroy him,"* possess a heart similar to the devil's. It is as if they lack a heart altogether, resembling those who profess to be Christians but act like ravenous wolves disguised in sheep's clothing.

15 Saul again sent messengers to see David, saying, "Bring me to bed so that I may kill him" (1 Samuel 19:15 KJV).

The devil hates you and desires to destroy you and everything you possess. He opposes God's children and all of God's creation. Ever since I arrived in this region, the enemy has attempted to attack me spiritually and mentally. The enemy uses some people to target you, which can prevent you from fulfilling your purpose here on Earth.

Take David, for example; he did nothing wrong except to be called by God to be King. The devil takes delight in placing someone from his kingdom of darkness in a position of authority—whether it's in jobs or ministries—God does not call that person. If that individual remains in such a position, they become a stumbling block, negatively influencing and hindering God's plan on Earth. This is why a child of God must occupy the most significant administrative roles, whether governmental, judicial, or legislative, so that God's plan for His kingdom can be fulfilled in the lives of many.

I faced significant struggles with the forces of darkness, which ultimately led to my removal from my previous job. At first, this seemed like a loss, but upon arriving at my new workplace, I discovered that when I mention I am a Christian, many people respond positively and treat me with kindness. If I had remained in my old job, I would have had to leave this region. However, because I was moved to a new position within the same base, I am now committed to staying here for about three more years, as 99% of the assignments last for three years. Since my supervisors recognized my character, they promised me an additional three years in this role.

Additionally, the radio application I submitted has been approved, allowing the word of God to be shared throughout this region. I have been granted three more years in a place from which the enemy wanted to remove me, but it was God who placed me here. During this time, I will continue to minister in this region, claiming what Jehovah has already declared alongside my pastor.

Furthermore, at the 7-Hour conference in 2023, while in the presence of Pastor Harrigan, an opportunity arose to establish radio stations across the United States. Since I will be here for three more years, I can continue to build the radio ministry that God entrusted to me in this local area and announce His kingdom on Earth.

This experience shows that everything works for good. Even though the enemy aimed to sideline me from my initial assignment, God used his actions to grant me favor with my superiors. Now, my pastor and I, along with River City Church, can spread the message of Christ's kingdom through FM radio 105.5, Jesus for the Nations.

28 And we know that all things work together for good to those who love God, to those who are called according to His purpose" (Rom 8:27 KJV).

God allowed the devil to test Job, and David was persecuted by Saul with the intent to kill him. Elijah faced persecution from Jezebel, Mordecai was despised, Joseph was sold into slavery, John was murdered, Peter denied Jesus, and our Savior, Jesus, was deliberately betrayed. In these stories, we observe two forces at work: one is the enemy using his tricks, and the other is our own flesh, which is our primary enemy.

It is widely understood that the enemy hates us and desires to see us dead; that is why diseases attack us. However, the most powerful adversary, for me, is our flesh. The enemy requires someone to manipulate our flesh and seeks to destroy God's purpose in our lives through it. We must learn to control our flesh, for it is often what leads to the downfall of many ministries. Peter faltered because of fear, which led him to deny Jesus, while Judas betrayed Him due to his love of money. Ultimately, the enemy relies on the flesh to carry out his plans effectively.

Do not become an accomplice to the devil by indulging in criticism or allowing your tongue to run unchecked; such behavior makes you a friend and instrument of the enemy.

CHAPTER 1
The War Between Two Worlds

Spiritual warfare is as real as the physical world we can see. This book is intended for those who desire a deeper intimacy with God and seek to win the battles between these two realms. It is for individuals who are weary of being distracted by the devil in the physical world and yearn to achieve their spiritual potential in both the physical and spiritual movements of God. These two worlds are in constant struggle, waging wars that, while often not visibly manifesting, are continuously at play and impact each other.

The Bible provides visions that illustrate the interaction between the spiritual and physical realms. For instance, Jesus mentions that heaven will be opened, and God's angels will ascend and descend upon Him (John 1:51). In the book of Daniel, a vision describes how dominion, glory, and a kingdom are given to one who appears to be a Son of Man (Daniel 7:13). In Matthew, Jesus asserts His authority over both heaven and earth (Matthew 28:18 NIV).

Additionally, the book of Revelation recounts how John, while in the spirit, heard a voice like a trumpet.

10 I was in the Spirit on the Lord's day, and I heard behind me a loud voice like a trumpet, 11 saying, "I am the Alpha and the Omega, the first and the last." Write down in a book what you see, and send it to the seven churches in Asia: to Ephesus, Smyrna, Pergamum, Thyatira, Sardis, Philadelphia, and Laodicea. (Revelation 1:10)

Throughout biblical history, there are numerous examples of angels intervening in the lives of human beings, such as the accounts of Hagar, Lot, and Abraham. These stories illustrate the close relationship between the spiritual and physical worlds and the divine assistance available to us. Spiritual maturity is essential for understanding and battling both physical and spiritual challenges.

Although Jesus Christ has already triumphed over evil, His followers must confront the forces of darkness in the world. It is crucial to remain alert and not allow the enemy to operate unchecked, keeping in mind that sickness does not belong to the Kingdom of Christ and that the gifts of healing are meant to restore health.

Moreover, we must recognize that our actions can impact the advancement of the Kingdom of God, either by aiding or hindering the efforts of those called to serve. It is vital to maintain communion and support our fellow believers, avoiding becoming obstacles to God's work. In this spiritual struggle, our greatest challenges may not come from external forces but rather from our own emotions and thoughts. The devil can use these aspects to mislead the children of light from their spiritual paths.

Therefore, it is essential to discern between the influences of light and darkness and to surround ourselves with those who walk in truth and light. In summary, this book encourages us to reflect on the reality of spiritual warfare, the significance of spiritual maturity, and the necessity of remaining vigilant and united in the fight against the forces of darkness.

CHAPTER 2

Entering The Spirit World Through Portals

The devil seeks to take possession of the earth and the heavens, but nothing can happen if the children of God do not allow it. The authority of the Father resides within us, and those who are in Him have the authority to subdue the powers on earth as it is in heaven. God has a plan and purpose for each of us on earth, just as He does in heaven. To embrace the plan of the Holy Spirit, individuals must confront the enemy of their lives: *"the flesh,"* and all that is under their influence, including the territories and boundaries of spiritual conflict.

"The earth is the Lord's, and the fullness thereof; the world and those who dwell in it" (Psalm 24:1). When a church rises in a location, it should not fight alone or against one another, but unite with other churches to take possession of the principalities and powers in that region. When government systems are used by Satan, it is the result of a prayerless church. Principalities are more powerful than regional ones, which are ruled by demons—who hold the lowest rank.

If you cannot drive out a demon, how can you confront a principality? This is why unity among churches, among believers, and within families is crucial. The covenant of agreement is essential for living a transformed life under the protection of more than two interceding for you, while you intercede for them. For instance, Daniel required the help of the archangel Michael because the level of region and assignment was significant to his calling. David needed Samuel, Elijah needed Elisha, Jesus needed His disciples, and Paul needed Silas.

> *"For we wrestle not against flesh and blood, but against principalities, against powers, against the rulers of the darkness of this world, against spiritual wickedness in high places"* (Ephesians 6:12). *"Two are better than one; because they have a good reward for their labor. For if they fall, one will lift up his companion; but woe to him who is alone; for when he falls, there is no one to lift him up. Again, if two lie down together, they will keep warm; but how can one be warm alone? If anyone overcomes one, two will withstand him; a threefold cord is not quickly broken"* (Ecclesiastes 4:9-12).

Principalities are the most powerful entities in a region, followed by powers and rulers, each having a specific level of authority. Therefore, churches must unite and resist the divisions that demons and the tools of the devil try to sow among them. Pastors must also be united at both the territorial and council levels.

As long as we are on earth, we are engaged in a covenant of spiritual conflict—a war for your life, your ministry, and those associated with you since before the foundation of the world. In this covenant, you are fully involved, whether you want to be or not, understanding that the authority of Christ is above all, including councils.

The wisdom of the Spirit and His revelation extend beyond merely being busy with church activities; they are linked to God's vision for this world, as written in His Word. Not only does this refer to the Bible, but also to your spoken words and decrees here on earth, which, when aligned with God's will, are created in the spiritual realm and manifested in the physical world.

Living Between Two Atmospheric Zones

As I looked out the window, I noticed that most of the trees that once provided me shade are now bare. All the leaves have died. The leaves do not fall on their own; rather, the tree sheds them when it needs energy and nutrients. The tree extracts all the energy from the leaves and discards them, as it no longer requires their presence.

In the same way, Jesus is the vine, and we are the branches. Without the vine, we are lifeless; the tree does not need us if we do not cling to it. If we do not understand the times, we will wither away. The tree needs its nutrients to endure the seasons; if it fails to utilize the nutrients in the leaves, it will lack sustenance.

Although the tree has water, air, and soil, the leaves are critical because they store essential nutrients. The tree gathers and extracts nutrients, knowing it has a reserve that prepares it for the dry and cold seasons ahead. You are a seed; it is up to you whether you will fight for the visibility of the trunks and leaves in the physical world. The seed requires depth and nutrients for its roots to grow strong.

> *12 For we wrestle not against flesh and blood, but against principalities, against powers, against the rulers of the darkness of this world, against spiritual wickedness in the heavenly places, (Ephesians 6:12). 9 Two are better than one; because they have better pay for their work. 10 For if they fall, the one will lift up his companion; but woe to the lonely! for when he falls, there will be no second to lift him up. 11 And if two sleep together, they shall warm one another; but how can a single one be heated? 12 And if any one prevail against one, two shall resist him; and a three-fold cord is not soon broken, (Ecclesiastes 4:9-12).*

The principalities are the largest of the regions, followed by the powers and rulers, each of which has its level. That is why the churches have to be united and not let those demons and the tools of the devil put division among them; the pastors must be united at the territorial and conciliar level.

As long as we are here on earth, we are engaged in a covenant of spiritual conflict, a war for your life and yours, for your ministry, and those who were involved with you before the foundation of the world. In this covenant, you are fully involved whether you want it or not, understanding that the authority of Christ is over all, including councils.

The wisdom of the Spirit and His revelation goes beyond a life full of things to do in the church, it links up with the vision of God here on earth, written by the law of the word, not just the Bible, but your word or your mouth and what you decree here on earth in the spiritual according to God's will is created in the supernatural world and manifested in the world, the physical world.

Likewise, everyone who is born of the Spirit needs to be guided and grow daily through Him. A leader who does not grow is a stagnant church, when someone comes to your church and has ministries, it is so that they grow together to build the whole church to fight against the enemy not against themselves, a person who fights among themselves is immature and has not submitted their emotions; emotions are good but uncontrolled emotions or controlled by the enemy separate friendships and are easy prey for the enemy.

If you don't have the strength, it's not the pastor's fault, is it, because you haven't understood that you're a tripartite being, what does that mean? That you are body, soul, and spirit. Your body needs the nourishing things of this physical world; your soul has to be directed by the spirit, that is, if you don't nourish it with spiritual food, it will die. Your soul connects with God through the Holy Spirit, your spirit is life, so a life of prayer is necessary, otherwise you will be direct easy prey for the enemy, especially when you spend your time filling up with television and the internet. You will become a tool in the hands of the enemy, that is, unclean spirits that will want to enter your body because the house is empty and neglected.

Lesson to learn: If God has confirmed you to stay in a church that is cold and powerless, and to die sitting spiritually, unused by God, and to have those gifts and the calling on your life go to waste then stay there! If anything inside you tells you, I know that God called me, and that He wants to use me in His Kingdom; then he seeks more of the Holy Spirit, of his confirmation and centralizes the priorities of the Kingdom. No pastor is going to get angry because God uses you. Especially in the call of Jehovah, who already predestined you before the foundation of the world. Always be prudent, wise, and submissive to God.

CHAPTER 3
Jehovah Will Be With His People

Most of the events you see today and hear about on the news are manipulated by a group of people who are influenced by the spirit of the antichrist. In this book, you are going to learn a lot about what happens around us, it is not an ordinary book; it is a book that will open both the physical and the spiritual senses. Don't be moved or intimidated by what you hear today or by what you see. While I was on a 21-day fast, God rested on me to read and study the book of Joel. The book of Joel speaks of the times to come, it is a prophetic book where, although it has only three chapters, it connects with the book of Revelation.

As I finished reading the first chapter of Joel, the Holy Ghost reminded me that these events are before the coming of our Lord Jesus Christ. It is also the great day of the Lord's wrath and the events of the seals that are spoken of in the book of Revelation, this will happen when the Lord unleashes his wrath on the face of the earth, we will not be here on earth, since those seals are for the wicked and disobedient.

> *Woe to the day! For the day of the Lord is near and will come as destruction from the Almighty (Joel 1:15).*

This day will be terrible, and Christ's church will not be present on earth. The book of Revelation speaks of the 144,000 sealed ones who come from the people of Israel.

Beloved, I want to tell you that what you are witnessing is being orchestrated by the Antichrist, who is already on earth and desires to reveal himself. That is why he uses governments and various institutions to control money, manipulate time, and create chaos. The so-called "climate of change" is merely a façade. There is no genuine climate change; instead, there is manipulation of the clouds and waters through devices designed to make the world believe that everything is coming to an end. Many people are deceived and remain asleep.

These events will be evident to those who will face the great and fearful day of the Lord that is approaching. The adversary seeks to hasten his kingdom on earth and rule as if he were Christ. The enemy knows the Scriptures; when Jesus was tempted, the devil quoted verses from the Bible.

> *He will command his angels to protect you, and they will hold you in their hands so that you will not stumble over any stone (Matthew 4:6).*

In the book of Joel, chapter one, Jehovah tells him, *"Awake."* This call to awaken is due to a numbness among the people, who struggle to identify God's timing. Verse six states, *"For a strong and innumerable people went up into my land; their teeth are like dandelions, and their molars are like lions."* This imagery is also echoed in Revelation 9:8.

This signifies that the church will face difficult times, yet Jehovah will be with His people. The events that will unfold in the coming months are manipulated by the Antichrist and the elite to accelerate his triumphal entry, purportedly bringing peace to Israel. The wars we observe today are being orchestrated to hasten the arrival of the Antichrist.

Do not despair about what you see and hear today. While the enemy may develop machines to manipulate time and seek to create human-robot beings or orchestrate conflicts between governments, he will never be able to recreate the true coming and rapture of the church, nor can he manipulate the bowls of God's wrath. Though the enemy may be well-versed in the prophecies of this time, he cannot know the future, as only Jehovah of armies understands His Kairos timing. Israel is God's clock, serving as His calendar.

The conflict that began in 2023, and which you may be reading about many years later, is an event manipulated by the Antichrist and his new world order. The book of Joel urges us to awaken, seek His presence, and remain vigilant in prayer and fasting.

The church should not wait for a tragic event to seek God through fasting or prayer; instead, you must pursue Him at all times. Perhaps the church has been passive, and it may seem that everything is going well, especially during the period when the Antichrist will establish peace for three and a half years. This time has yet to be seen.

God's Kairos time cannot be manipulated by humans or elite agendas. Yes, we are living in the last days, perilous times, but this is not what the Bible refers to in terms of birth pains or the bowls described in the book of Revelation. Everything you observe is being manipulated by men; it is not yet the genuine time of God, as God's timing cannot be altered by anyone.

CHAPTER 4
Oath of Allegiance

Our American military is based on the *"Oath of Allegiance."* I work in the armed forces of the United States, yes, in the army there are many people with diverse characters as in any other job, we train together as individuals we are very diverse, but we are recognized as the same as the characteristics based on teaching, whether in our walk, talk, act, we are very similar in the form of training; we have regulations that mold us to think in a certain way and manner; we teach seven values that we govern when we enter the military, the value of Leadership: Loyalty, Integrity, duty, respect, putting the other before you, honor, personal value. These characteristics must be inside a soldier. A soldier is faithful and loyal, has integrity, and does not seek his own, but always seeks to help others. A soldier in Christ's army is courageous; he is not afraid, he puts his trust in the Lord. Job, however upright he was, came to him what he feared.

"What I feared most came to me; What scared me the most happened to me." (Job 3:25 NIV)

Your flesh is afraid of something, and that something, satan knows, and he will use it one day against you, so we need to understand that the flesh is the one that must be subdued so that the enemy, when he comes, cannot destroy us, and be firm until the end. The Bible says that we have an adversary, our enemy "Satan," where we know that this world has a spiritual struggle in the heavenly places, but the biggest battles we face, and most of the time, are within the church. Our greatest battle begins in our minds. In this book, we will talk about the two worlds and their differences.

The enemy frequently attacks your mind, seeking to destroy your character and make you feel like a loser, walking around with your head down as if you have done something wrong. The devil has always aimed to turn God's creation into a defeat; his jealousy is widespread across the earth. Eve sinned because of what the enemy placed in her path—what he told her and what she chose to believe: *"You will be like God."* This curiosity led her to disobedience, causing her to lose sight of God's plan. Remember, faith comes from hearing the word of God, not the lies of the enemy. When the enemy tries to speak to you, it's important to close every door he might use to enter your mind and influence you

Prayer: Father, may I not be easily manipulated and influenced by the enemy, nor be frightened by what I see or hear. because I do not give in to fear, because fear is not God.

Between Two Worlds By Elizabeth Walcott

Preparation and the call

Every soldier before fighting is first called, he is prepared, and then he is sent with orders, he enlists in the army, according to his level, branch and academy of category that is how he is exercised, that is, if he is from the air, sea, territorial force, that's how they train him. Likewise, the one who enters into a spiritual war has to be equipped by the Holy Spirit and have the whole armor of God. If you do not have the Holy Spirit, you will not be able to live a full and victorious life; without the Holy Spirit, the hosts of evil will have you in defeat.

Therefore, it is essential that a Soldier knows what he is getting into, who his war is with, what artillery the enemy has, and if he has all the equipment to be able to win this war, and if he does not have it, he prepares, acquires knowledge to be able to defeat the enemy, to know the weaknesses, tools, connections to be able to defeat him.

There is no Christian, no disciple who says he has a victorious life and does not pray; every man and woman of God who has a life in victory knows that it has not been easy to stay there. We cannot enter a war without first being equipped, without first knowing your enemy, without first knowing and knowing their territory. When a soldier is empowered by God, he understands the tools of the kingdom of God. Consequently, he equips himself with new tools, reflecting his training levels and rank.

A private person cannot be given responsibility for cybernetic tools without first studying them; every level depends on their rank and profession. As they rise in rank, so does their level of responsibility and stature of rank. A private is not given a Company of Soldiers; if the rank or level is not suitable for that rank, the Captain is the one who is the commander of a unit, not the private.

The first battle I want you to focus on is the battlefield in the mind. On this battlefield that is similar to a sponge absorbing everyone around us, our eyes sometimes make mistakes in thinking that the people in front of us are the enemy. Our ears also hear things. Eve listened to the serpent and then analyzed what the serpent told her. That is why the Lord says that we must renew our minds daily.

That's why there are different voices that speak to us on a daily basis, we have the voice of the Holy Spirit, who is eager to speak to us, who is completely open to speak to our lives, but now until we close every voice that is out there, we will not be able to fully understand the battlefield that we are with two different worlds. But in the spiritual world, they deal with our senses and enter into those who are weaker.

Every worldly spirit, demons, powers, hosts of wickedness know you, they recognized Jesus; soon Jesus got out of the boat, this young man ran and fell on Jesus' feet.

In today's preaching, the Lord moved in a special way, He taught us that we have a physical world as well as a spiritual world. We know that, in this physical world, spiritual things are not yet seen, but in the spiritual world, when we pray, something is happening. We may not see it with our own physical eyes, but those who have their spiritual eyes open will be able to see it.

Be a Warrior in Training

In the age we live in, it's easy to fall into the pattern of worry and passive living. We often cling to Bible verses and ideologies from our ancestors that keep us in a state of passivity, instead of encouraging us to fight for our own freedom. While some may stand up and battle for what is right, others prefer to enjoy the sacrifices made by those who fight.

Life is tough; nothing worth having comes for free. Take David, for instance. As a shepherd, God prepared him for battle. When bears and lions threatened his sheep, David didn't run away; he faced these challenges head-on. Ultimately, when it was time to demonstrate his skills, he stood against Goliath, the largest giant of all. In today's world, we too must confront the evil forces around us. We must not settle for a mediocre mindset, as the Bible warns us about complacency in the end times.

Many of us agree that we are "living in the end times," but that does not mean we should stop fighting for what belongs to us. This land is our inheritance; God granted us full dominion after the resurrection of the second Adam, Jesus Christ. As the church, we often lie dormant, accommodating the enemy as long as we are left undisturbed. Many proclaim, "God is going to return," or "We are living in the last days!" I refer to this as "justification." We find it easier to justify our cold, stagnant spiritual lives rather than take action.

When Elijah faced a threat from Queen Jezebel, he fled, leading to moments of silence and distance from God. Similarly, we often desire ease; we want others to fight and pray for us, and once victory is achieved, we take the credit, claiming, "I knew God had already won the victory." We rationalize our failures and let others engage in battles on our behalf, taking credit for the efforts of individuals like Martin Luther King Jr. Not everyone agreed with him, but many celebrated the achievements that followed.

Some may say, "Jesus paid it all," forgetting that "the kingdom of God suffers violence, and only the violent take it by force." Nothing in this world is born without purpose. Matthew 11:12 (KJV) states, "And from the days of John the Baptist until now, the kingdom of heaven suffers violence, and the violent take it by force."

Throughout history, people have enjoyed the benefits that resulted from struggles, yet the spiritual preparation that nurtured those victories has often been overlooked. God unleashed His Spirit and revealed His purpose on Earth. You and I are destined to claim nations, kingdoms, and dominions.

In October 2022, I attended a lecture by Pastor Juan Harrigan called "7 Hours in His Presence." Over 4,000 people gathered from around the globe, some driving 36 hours to receive healing and leave transformed. Many waited in line for over eight hours, arriving as early as 1:00 AM just to secure a closer seat to the pulpit.

The power of God was evident in a way I had never experienced before; we felt His fire in our faces and bodies. Healing and liberation were manifested in the lives of thousands. When I asked God why we don't see such power in our churches, He replied, *"Because my people came with the expectation of receiving something from Me, and I am here for them to receive it."* As stated in 2 Chronicles 5:14 (KJV),

> *"So the priests could not stand to minister because of the cloud, for the glory of the Lord had filled the house of God."*

We must begin with faith and expectation, preparing to receive something powerful from God. We need to release everything that distracts us so we can hear His voice. This transformation stems from a recent revival where God ministered to my life and many others. When you listen for God's voice, you remain alert to what He wants to convey to you, your nation, and the world.

We do not fight against flesh and blood!

When you enter a new stage of your growth, it doesn't mean that your giants are going to leave; If you confront us at that moment, you will have to face them later. Since the enemy is not interested in stopping you where you are, but in stopping you so that you do not get where God wants to take you and achieve your purpose in the Kingdom of Christ. The enemy is interested in paralyzing yourself, blocking you, and killing your call. For many years he has been robbing God's people, killing the destiny of many, putting them in mental and emotional cages, where many have died by the mouth of someone who spoke ill of them for letting themselves be dominated by emotions.

The enemy fights you when you decide to continue against the winds and tempests that he sends, or believes in your path, while you are paralyzed you are not interested in him, but when you decide *"I am going to do the will of God here on earth, serve God in the gift that He has given me"* A war is unleashed against you and yours, therefore a soldier is not afraid, he stands on a war footing and puts on the whole armor of Jehovah.

God spoke to me through Pastor Harrigan two Sundays ago, and this Sunday, he tells me again through my pastor Reece that you're going to have to face those giants when you're going to do something great for God. Do not be afraid that people who you would never imagine will rise up against you and your ministry.

Spiritual warfare is real, the earthly world and the spiritual world are real, they are not Ada stories, nor stories from TV movies, they are real. The Bible speaks of a demon-possessed boy in the book of Luke.

> *37 The next day, when they came down from the mountain, a large crowd came out to meet them. 38 And behold, a man of the crowd cried out, saying, Teacher, please see my son, for he*

is the only one I have; 39 And it comes to pass that a spirit takes him, and suddenly cries out, and shakes him violently, and makes him foam, and spoiling, he hardly departs from him. 40 And I begged your disciples to cast him out, but they could not. 41 Jesus answered and said, "O unbelieving and perverse generation! How long shall I be with you, and endure you? Bring your son here. 42 And as the boy approached, the demon struck him down and shook him violently; but Jesus rebuked the unclean spirit, and healed the boy, and restored him to his father. 43 And they were all amazed at the greatness of God, (Luke 9:37-43).

We must open our eyes when we are dealing with diseases, the enemy is cunning in using his demons to send diseases into our lives, this boy had demons and foamed at the mouth. There are demons that get inside people, and operate in the legality of the human being, when you open the doors to the enemy, satan uses that door to enter. When Jesus rebukes these spirits, they recognize power and authority.

Satan sends spirits that lull you to sleep or keep you entertained, so when you want to pray or read the Bible, you get very sleepy. But when you listen to your favorite movies, you don't get sleepy! Satan is going to send his demonic spirits to keep you defeated or to live a passive life in God, so that you don't come to the full filling of the Spirit, and you don't fulfill God's purpose here on earth as in the spirit world. When you are going through sickness or some spiritual chill against you, it is not because God does not want to use you, it is because satan has sent demons into your house so that your house will be destroyed, or so that your children, your wife or your husband are spiritually asleep.

That's why most Christians are sick; diseases are not cast out with oils, those demons that are stalking you, or your house, those demons come out with the power of the Word, in the name of Jesus, and fasting and prayer. The demons recognize authority. When you have the power of the Father, the demons know you, they knew Jesus and his power, and Paul and Peter. When we are intimate with God and filled with His power, demons have to submit to God's authority in you, through Jesus who lives within you.

But some of the Jews, itinerant exorcists, tried to call on the name of the Lord Jesus on those who had evil spirits, saying, *"I adjure you by Jesus, the one who preaches Paul."*

> *14 There were seven sons of a certain Sceva, a Jew, chief priest, who did this. 15 But the evil spirit answered and said, "I know Jesus, and I know who Paul is; but who are you? 16 And the man in whom the evil spirit was, leaping upon them and overpowering them, was stronger than they, so that they fled from that house naked and wounded (Acts 19:13-15).*

The war between the children of God and the children of darkness is very real. Some people are demonized or influenced, and the spirits have their mouths silenced and their ears deaf, and it is because the devil has silenced them so that they do not pray effectively. Satan has tried to intimidate me at work; there are many witches and Satanists here in this place. I have seen how they have risen against me.

But the power of Jehovah is greater. Jesus sent me to this place, and I refuse to be taken out of here. The devil has power, but Jesus is almighty. Nothing and no one will be able to stand against you if the power of Jehovah is with you. They will all fall at Jesus' feet and submit to the Lord of hosts.

Let us pray: Eternal Father you have created me in your image therefore I have your authority and I represent you here on earth, just as I am seated in heavenly places together with Christ, so I decree and declare that word today in my life, my house, my neighborhood and all that I contribute and find myself against me, It is ruled by the power of the name of Jesus, who is the owner and all-powerful of all things visible and invisible (Ephesians 2:6 KJV).

CHAPTER 5
The Power of His Name

Our parents gave us our names, although many of us don't like them; that's the one they gave us at birth. The surname is one of the most important, which is why parents recognize their children and give them an inheritance. Each name has a meaning. God is intentional, Numbers 11:24-25. The kingdom of heaven suffers violence, and only the mighty take it away; this puts the people it snatches into a category of the brave. Violent people snatch; you have a special DNA.

Sarah did not give birth because she was connected to the Babylonian system, so God took her out of there, and she became pregnant because of the power of God. We must disconnect from Babylon. Many do not give birth, because they are connected to Babylon. God takes you out of the Babylonian system. The fact that God sends you to a place of famine doesn't mean that God isn't there. God allows that to break that system, but ask Joseph.

"But when it pleased God, He took me away from my mother's womb, and called me by His grace."

Daniel is known as a major prophet, just like Elijah and Jeremiah. These men of God went through prisons, persecutions, he the Bible we know his daily life, Daniel prayed every day three times, Elijah went into the mountain to pray for hours and days, Moses was raised adopted by Pharaoh's daughter, but God allowed his own mother to raise him, he killed a soldier, David slept with someone else's wife; but that didn't stop God from using it.

Today's celebrities, such as Michael Jordan, had to fight to get where they are. Michael Jordan is on Wikipedia because of his fame.

God sets us apart for ministry, and God constitutes the ministry and the calling. The anointing comes upon us for something great that God wants to do here on earth, and many times the enemy wants to destroy your purpose and your anointing, to divert you from your purpose. How, for example, when David had to face enemies, even his son Absalom.

The Seed

The state of the flower depends on the soil and the environment. If the flower has dead leaves, it is because the soil has not been providing its nutrients, and the sun is absent. The flower needs to have all the nutrients in order to survive, just as the flower, all of us need God and His word. If we don't pray and search the scriptures very soon, we will be like a dead flower.

Each fruit reproduces according to its seed. Listening to Dr. Vandana Shiva she talked about how Bill Gates is collecting the seeds and destroying the rest of the seeds, making GMOs; this very rich man is experimenting with God, he is destroying the cattle, the crops and the crops of the farmers, but Dr. Vandana Shiva is also collecting the seeds because she knows how important reproduction is.

I want to clarify something, in this world there are good and bad people, I have been able to see how demons have taken over the bodies of the delegates who are in power, as well as many millionaires who hate God and his creation, with the excuse that the world is overpopulated and humanity must be destroyed.

In the physical world, these men are atheists, millionaires who want to erase everything that resembles God. In the book of Genesis, God said, *"Bring forth the green grass, the grass that yields seed; a tree of fruit that bears fruit according to its kind."* That's why this doctor has waged war on Bill Gates, because she says she's not going to let him destroy what is ours, it's already created to eat and live to feed man.

To us, I say to us because they are throwing us from the sky in airplanes, chemicals to control the weather and kill vegetation, one of those chemicals is the chemical antifreeze that they are for cars, it is composed of nitrogen, and it is harmful to our system and plants. The government pays the CID more than 500 million a year by using planes with chemicals to destroy and manipulate vegetation and the climate. These chemicals make the seas, lakes, plants dry up, it also controls the climate, and farmers are burning their farms and taking them away if they don't pay attention, they also make their chemicals in the land, which produces diseases and controls the products that are born, which means that instead of fertilizer for the land they add chemicals that they have, Genetically Modified Organisms (GMOs), this chemical destroys your immune system to bring disease into your system, many products are synthetic.

Something that the devil does not want to realize is that the Bible says, "And it was so." The only one who can create and reproduce effectively without manipulation of science is God. "God said," and it was so; when God does something, he does it well. "And God saw that all things were good" of Jehovah is the earth and its fullness and all that dwells in it, (Psalm 24:1).

The End Times Prayer

In the book of Genesis, chapter 18:23-25 it says,

23 Abraham came and said, "Will you also destroy the righteous with the wicked?" 24 Perhaps there are fifty righteous people within the city: will you also destroy, and will you not spare the place, no matter how fifty righteous people are within it? 25 Far be it from thee to do such that you put the righteous to death with the wicked, and that the righteous be treated as the wicked; never do so. Is not the judge of all the earth to do what is right?

Between Two Worlds By Elizabeth Walcott

I love how Abraham intercedes for the city. Let not the righteous pay for the wicked. It gives me a pain in my gut when we pray without revelation, *"God has mercy on the world."* NO, that's not how you pray, let's learn to pray like this prophet, "Abraham". Today, there is passivity; people only say... *We are in the end times!* Yes, but David, when he heard of the uncircumcised Philistine, did not say; Oh, I'm going to pray and watch God move and He's going to help us destroy that uncircumcised one. No! David put on the power of God and cut off the head of that uncircumcised man. Esther didn't say, I'm going to pray and fast, and then I'll see what God is going to do! No, it was so, God used Joshua and Caleb to become spies to see the land that they were going to conquer, then they saw "with spiritual eyes" and gave that word of conquest to Moses and Aron. They went in and conquered the land.

There are times when the Holy Spirit is going to disturb you because He has a strategic plan like Esther. She prayed and fasted with her concubines, and prayer and fasting saved the people. (Esther 5:2) When the king saw Esther in the courtyard in royal robes, the word says that Esther had grace before the king's eyes.

Today there should be pastors, prophets, evangelists at the door of the presidencies, asking to speak with the Presidents, so that all those large mega churches stop so much satanic pedophilia, they should be every day in appointment with the legislators, in the palaces, to exhort and direct those who govern, Where are those great churches that are not outside helping the people?

The United States has to give an account to God for the so much pedophilia and morbidity that exists. Today, we see many protests of incoherent and lies-ridden people in the street protesting things that do not make sense and have not been put into God's legitimate plan. And those tenants fight for unheard-of and absurd rights, laws changed by governments under the influence of the devil, and for them those laws are reality, that is evidence that violence is the weapon of those who are not right, on the contrary, God and the protests of the churches that have been made in the past, they are peaceful and with concrete and basic results for the family, the people and freedom. Let us pray like this, Father, Jehovah of hosts, do your will, here.

Led by the Holy Spirit

After the intercessory group, listening to the preaching, the pastor was talking about Joshua, and while I was praying one morning and listening to Pastor Harrigan, who was talking about "Get away from the wrong people," it was about 6 AM. The preaching was about the sin of Achan, in the book of Joshua (7:10 [KJV]). That same morning, my child got up and told me that his devotional had been about Joshua and Achan in the book of Joshua, chapter 7. When we are led by the Holy Spirit, God speaks to us and shows us His will. We have to be careful who we introduce into the ministry. God knows everything we do, and others do.

Beware of the Achan who will make you lose in war. Achan's sin caused God's people to lose the battle against the enemies. The wrong people who come into your life and don't want to help you in ministry, or care about what God is doing in your life, or your ministry. We must remove sin as Joshua removed Achan. I would like to help and educate the Achans, but unfortunately, God sometimes commands us to remove people from our lives because they are an Achan that obstructs everything. They block your blessing; therefore, remove everything that doesn't let you grow because they don't believe in the vision God has given you.

Prayer reveals to you the will of the Father, and intimate prayer with God anticipates what is going to happen in the world and in your life. When David prayed for direction on how to proceed against his enemies, Jehovah would come and speak to him. Moses prayed to Yahweh when the people needed direction; we still see that God often approached Moses to tell him what the people were doing.

I remember being approached by a boy who said that God had told him that I was his wife and he wanted to marry me, but I told him that I needed direction from God to confirm if that was the case. Several months passed and God showed me a dream where I saw myself with my son in a forest running, calling him, because my work called me to do my work as a soldier, but I saw the boy from a distance in the sky only his face looking at me, and God showed me that the boy was not going to support me with my son or with my work.

Beware of the stagnant! Many hide with the phrase "Christ is coming soon." We are in the end times." The enemy has used many with that phrase where they have sat comfortably and excused their spiritual cooling of prayer and activation in ministry, I don't want you to misunderstand me. The difference is when someone uses that phrase as an excuse, and they're not active in the ministry God has given them here to counter the forces of the enemy. They are seated and everything is based on that phrase; instead of seeking how to be a hammer or tools in the hands of Jehovah for the destruction of strength against the kingdom of darkness. A life without prayer is no life, no power, no Father's fulfilled purpose for the earth with that person.

Spiritual Warfare

Evil spirits operate based on the words you speak; they latch onto your language, creating an open door for the enemy. This is why some people struggle to articulate themselves and feel stagnant in their progress. It's not that the enemy is attacking them directly; rather, just as faith comes through hearing and confessing the word of God, the enemy infiltrates your mind through dishonest words.

Those who frequently complain and gossip can inadvertently empower these negative forces. Many fail to control and can inadvertently empower these negative forces. Many fail to control their tongues and do not fear God when they speak ill of others. In the spiritual realm, forces are at work that contradict and oppose God's will. Satan's kingdom actively battles against Jehovah's kingdom.

The enemy seeks to claim something that does not belong to him: the earth. This world was created by God for us to inhabit and thrive within it. Therefore, we cannot afford to become complacent or take a spiritual break; we must remain vigilant at all times. We are engaged in a spiritual battle, one that is unseen but manifests in the physical realm, where demons and principalities conspire to attack us and watch us falter. These demons are organized and listen to every plan we make, attempting to thwart God's purpose in our lives.

This is why we must pray and fast before embarking on any new endeavor or setting goals for ourselves. The enemy wants to disrupt our plans and undermine our happiness as we pursue God's purpose here on earth. To triumph in these spiritual battles, it is essential to know who we are. We will not be consumed by the enemy's attacks. Just as David faced challenges in 2 Samuel 5:17-25, we too find ourselves in constant warfare in the face of giants and troubles.

The term "Refaim" appears in biblical, Ugaritic, and Phoenician texts, referring to a people known for their great stature (Genesis 14:5; 15:20; Deuteronomy 2:11). When giants appear, it often signifies that God is preparing to elevate us in our ministry. Their presence is a reminder that great things are on the horizon, and we are destined for something significant from God.

These giants are confronted by tying them up and stripping them of their strongholds through the Word. Exalt the Lord and remember the prophetic promises He has already given you in the face of those giants. Let them know who called you and instituted you in your calling and ministry. Even if your giants are sicknesses, use the promises and covenants that Jehovah has spoken about your life.

Since you have a promise from Jehovah, don't leave until He fulfills that word. David was called and anointed by Jehovah as king, and he faced enemies and giants. However, he knew how to pray and receive strength in the presence of God, waiting strategically under the guidance of the Holy Spirit.

When the Philistines heard that David had been anointed king over Israel, they came to find him. When David became aware of this, he went down to the fortress, and the Philistines scattered themselves in the Valley of Rephaim. David inquired of the Lord, asking whether he should go up against the Philistines and if God would deliver them into his hands. The Lord said to David, "Go up, for I will deliver the Philistines into your hands." David went to Baal-perazim and defeated them, declaring, "The Lord has made a breach between my enemies before me, like a breach of water." That is why he called the place Baal-perazim.

The Philistines forsook their idols there, and David and his men took them away. Subsequently, the Philistines regrouped and scattered themselves again in the Valley of Rephaim. When David inquired of the Lord again, He instructed him not to go up directly but to take a detour behind them and to confront them in front of the balsam trees. God told him,

> *"When you hear the sound of marching in the tops of the balsam trees, then you will act quickly, for the Lord will have gone out before you to strike the army of the Philistines."*

David followed the Lord's command and smote the Philistines from Geba to Gezer.

God is about to manifest His glory like never before; His power and authority will be demonstrated throughout the earth. A powerful wave of healing and deliverance is being released in the atmosphere, and you can feel its presence as never before. You have been chosen to witness this unparalleled power, which cannot be stopped by any demon or evil force; nothing and no one can hinder the Almighty Yahweh.

As it is written,

"And the Egyptians shall know that I am the Lord when I glorify myself in Pharaoh, in his chariots, and in his horsemen" (Exodus 14:18).

The Lord said to Moses, "Lift up your rod." When God goes before us, we can be assured that we will overcome and win the battles we face. God purposely hardened Pharaoh's heart so that He could glorify Himself and show the nations confronting Israel that Jehovah was with them.

While I was going about my daily routines, I found myself in a battlefield where my boss was being used by the enemy. When I got home, the first thing my child said to me was, "Thou hast set a table before me in the presence of my troublemakers" (Psalm 23:5 KJV). God spoke to me and confirmed that He is going to prepare tables before your enemies.

Between Two Worlds By Elizabeth Walcott

Living between two worlds

I observed a tree outside my window that had lost all its leaves. What must the leaf feel, as its purpose is to be on the tree, not on the ground? This mirrors how we sometimes feel—we are meant for stability, to have a family and stable work, or even thriving businesses for a secure future. Yet, unexpected changes can pressure us to leave our comfortable and stable environments. Situations arise that are beyond our control, forcing us to FALL.

I don't know about you, but praying and seeking God has become a challenge for me. At times, I feel overwhelmed—things seem to fall apart each week. I must continually push forward to lead this Christian life.

Prayer has become a pressure and a push toward something that sometimes feels too strong. Jesus taught me something very important today, and I want to share it with you. I want you to read this, that Jesus reminded me that when he stood before Pilate and had the first choice of being delivered by the people choosing between him, or a thief, thug, and murderer "Barabbas," (Matthew 27:20-23).

Those who rose up against Jesus were the same religious hypocrites that we often have in front of us, whether at work or even within the church. But that's not all Jesus showed me today! I had something similar, a similar situation, where people are going to turn against you, especially bosses and co-workers. And what happened here?

It is a basis of laws of territories, when you have an assignment, that is, God has called us to conquer territories, the enemy will want to take your territory. Example: The Lord anointed David king, and a Saul arose; Joseph as Pharaoh's blessing and right-hand man in Egypt in time of drought, and Potiphar's wife (Gen 39:7-18) arose with slander to bring Joseph out of a place where Jehovah had already promised him. This is how the enemy will rise up when you are in a certain region and physical place, so that they will not dislodge him and all his followers. The enemies of the past were physical, the enemies of the present are spiritual and physical. Be filled and clothed with the power of the Holy Spirit.

CHAPTER 6
Christ, Change Your Name

Feelings can sometimes rob us of blessings, and parents are often guided by the circumstances of life. When a husband leaves, it can affect how parents treat their children or grandchildren. This is particularly true when grandparents are responsible for raising them; sometimes, they may struggle to express affection, while grandchildren often know how to show love. I was called "foolish" throughout my childhood, as my mother frequently labeled me that way. Yet, from a young age, I felt destined for something greater. I loved going to church, even though my parents did not attend. In the Bible, we read about Jabez in 1 Chronicles. His name means "pain," reflecting the sorrow surrounding his birth. The scripture states:

> "8 Kos begat Anub, Zobeba, and the family of Aharhel the son of Harum. 9 And Jabez was more illustrious than his brothers, whom his mother called Jabez, saying, Because I bore him in sorrow," 1 Chronicles 4:8-9.

Being named for hardship does not mean that Jabez had to be a source of pain. Instead, Jehovah changes our names to reflect strength and courage rather than fear.

The Battle Between Two Worlds: Strategy

In the spiritual realm, there are forces that attack our Christian brothers and sisters. The Bible reminds us that we have an adversary, Satan. We understand that there are minds influenced by this world that can affect heavenly matters, yet the most significant battles often occur within the church itself. Consider the armed forces: the greatest battles start in the physical realm, and various branches rely on one another; the Air Force needs the army, the army needs the Navy, and the Navy requires the Marines. The National Guard collaborates with other military divisions, all working together toward common goals. This book explores the spiritual battle between these two realms—the physical and spiritual worlds. Spiritual unity occurs when the angels of Jehovah join us in our fight against spiritual challenges. Therefore, the Church must stand together in unity, regardless of size or location, acknowledging that all ministries must work collaboratively for the advancement of the Kingdom.

The first battle I want to focus on is the battlefield of the mind. This mental battlefield acts like a sponge, absorbing everything around us and everything our eyes see. There is a spirit of persuasion that contaminates our thoughts, leading us to mistakenly believe that the person in front of us is our enemy. Our ears may interpret things negatively, causing us to misjudge what we hear in our daily lives.

Daily, we encounter various voices speaking to us; however, we also have the Holy Spirit, who eagerly wants to communicate with us and can help remove these conflicting voices. Until we manage to silence every external influence, we will struggle to fully comprehend this battlefield. We are caught in a conflict between two different worlds, which creates a barrier in both the physical and spiritual realms. The spirit world presents various levels of spiritual beings that we must confront. If we cannot contend with the weaker spirits that attack our minds, like the demons that affected the Gadarene demoniac, who ran to Jesus as soon as He stepped off the boat, how can we hope to fight at a higher level? God without space or limits

So Jacob left Beersheba and went to Haran

11 And he came to a certain place, and slept there, for the sun had already set; and he took of the stones of that place and placed it at its head, and lay down in that place. 12 And he dreamed: and behold, a ladder was leaning on the ground, and its end touched the heavens; and behold, angels of God ascended and descended through it. 13 And behold, the LORD was on the top of it, who said, "I am the LORD, the God of Abraham your father, and the God of Isaac; The land on which you are lying I will give to you and to your descendants. Genesis 28:10-13

Some portals open when you pray; your words enter that realm and create miracles, bring deliverance, and can even change systems of government. This is exemplified by Jesus and the story of the

Gadarene, where He cast out all the demons and brought freedom to the man. Similarly, Jacob connected with God through prayer, which opened a portal and changed his destiny—his name was even changed according to God's plan. God is limitless and has no boundaries; He cares about your business, your family, and your life. God is interested in everything you do, the psalmist said

> *"Where shall I escape from Thy presence?" Where shall I go from Thy Spirit, or whither shall I flee from Thy presence?"(Proverbs 15:3) The eyes of the LORD are everywhere, watching the evil and the good" (Isaiah 29:15).*

Even if you find yourself in a closet, the Lord is there. Even while you are sleeping, He is watching over you and taking care of you. When the devil plans to harm you, God may wake you up at dawn to pray and thwart the enemy's schemes. This is why it is very important to pray when God awakens you early; take a few minutes to pray, as something may be about to happen, and you may be called to intercede for that situation.

In the Scriptures, angels appeared to Abraham when they were on a mission to destroy Sodom and Gomorrah. Because God did not hide His intentions from Abraham, he was able to intercede for those cities. Abraham's response was to serve the angels and to inquire about their purpose. The Lord revealed to Abraham the promise He had for him and simultaneously disclosed what He planned to do in Sodom and Gomorrah. Abraham is depicted as a powerful intercessor in the Bible, successfully saving his nephew Lot and Lot's daughters

(Genesis 18). When God calls you to pray, it is not only for your own needs but also for the welfare of your community. God, along with His angels, is discussing what He intends to do in our lives and the world around us. This is why God has no boundaries or limitations.

The Angelic Visit

During a ministerial meeting, I experienced a profound presence of God while we engaged in the farewell prayer. Bishop Merrit invited Bishop Jakes Givan to lead us in prayer, but as we prayed, God's presence was so overwhelming that we could not conclude with a simple prayer. His glory was felt so intensely that we were all filled with His presence. It was as if someone had entered the room, but I knew it was not a human presence—it was the angels of Jehovah. I opened my eyes, expecting to see someone, but there was no one there. The sense of God's presence was so powerful that we began to glorify His name by speaking in tongues. The Lord has been revealing to me that He is going to pour out His presence mightily in these end times, as prophesied in the book of Joel.

> *"And after this I will pour out my Spirit on all flesh, and your sons and your daughters shall prophesy; your old men will dream dreams, and your young people will see visions. 29 And I will pour out my Spirit on the male and female servants in those days" (Joel. 2:28-29).*

Sin

Between Two Worlds By Elizabeth Walcott

The man born of a woman, short of days, and weary of trouble, comes forth like a flower and is cut off, Job 14:1.

Only those who have a purpose from God and have not done much with their lives are experiencing the most difficulty. It doesn't take much to make life challenging; simply being born brings its own set of problems. We can look at our best example, Jesus, our King. His time on earth was brief; he began his ministry at the age of thirty and was crucified just three years later.

So, why do bad things happen to good people? When we are born, we enter a beautiful world. Our parents introduce us to a life filled with toys and family, and we celebrate holidays that seem to bring everyone joy. Yet, we often face hardships that can feel overwhelming. Our loved ones suffer from illness, we experience divorce, debt, and sometimes we struggle to put food on the table or have any money in our pockets. Relationships can crumble, as spouses leave for others, and we watch helplessly as loved ones battle cancer and other debilitating illnesses.

What have we done to deserve this? It was "Eve who sinned," not me! If she and her husband Adam, made the mistake, why must I suffer the consequences? It might seem as straightforward as that, but the reality is much more complex. In the military, for instance, we employ a system of *"maximum punishment."* When a soldier misbehaves, we use that incident as a lesson for others to discourage similar actions. We train soldiers to develop character, discipline, and resilience in preparation for the challenges they may face.

Likewise, our Heavenly Father teaches us that life requires bravery. Everything we see around us will one day be destroyed, Matthew 24:1: *"Not one stone will be left upon another that will not be thrown down".* Our Lord Jesus Christ also reassures us of this truth.

> *"These things I have spoken to you, that in me you may have peace. In the world you will have affliction; but be of good cheer, I have overcome the world" (John 16:33).*

The Bible also says

16 For the Lord himself will descend from heaven with a shout, with the voice of the archangel, and with the trumpet of God; and the dead in Christ will rise first. 17 Then we who are alive and remain will be caught up with them in the clouds to meet the Lord in the air, and so we will always be with the Lord." 1 Thessalonians 4:16:17

In other words, all is not lost; we will be reunited with our loved ones when the Lord Jesus resurrects them, and we will live with Jesus forever. Even if they don't recognize us or we don't recognize them, our hope is to find ourselves in a joyful place that aligns with God's original plan for "Adam and Eve."

There will be a new earth and a new heaven, as described in the book of Revelation. The Bible teaches that we are seated with Christ in heavenly places, together with Him.

"And with him he raised us up, and also made us sit in the heavenly places with Christ Jesus" (Ephesians 2:6).

CHAPTER 7

The Price

In the year 2020, the earth suffered terrible news, and I refer to the earth because it was the whole world that suffered from an outbreak and threat of death, in that a deadly virus was unleashed that devastated many, regardless of the social class status of each individual. In the month of December, close to Easter, I had a dream where I saw my uncle Rogelio, the youngest of all my uncles, little boy came to visit me in Germany, I looked for him at the airport, and I saw that he did not have a suitcase, and I asked him, "Uncle, where is your suitcase?" and he replied that he did not bring a suitcase but only his change of clothes.

I didn't take it seriously because my uncle was seen as the black sheep of the house, I thought he didn't have money to buy a suitcase, then I asked him if he was hungry, he said yes, I told him, let's eat something here at the airport, we joined a long line, where they were selling food, And suddenly I see that my uncle is at the front of the line, and that he is helping the cashier, which by the way happened to be people giving my uncle money to help him in line.

In the dream, I saw a few coins in his hands, but it was something he was earning for helping the cashier with the orders. When I woke up from the dream I understood that something was going to happen to my uncle, this dream was like two days before Christmas, I prayed for him and during Christmas I called my family and asked them where my uncle is, that, if you have seen him, have you talked to him?

I told them to contact him, that I had a dream about him, and I didn't like it. On January 3, my family received a call from the neighbors that the house where my uncle is smelled very bad, they called the police, and they found my uncle dead several days ago.

When I received that news, I broke down very hard because my uncle had been beaten and died alone in the house. I felt very anguished because I thought that, in his last moments, he wanted to call someone, and no one listened to him. Perhaps he asked God to tell someone about his condition, in his last breaths, he cried out to God that the angels tell someone to meet him in the house. That angel was me, and I could not do anything, since I was far from the country.

I know that I could blame my family for not having looked for him when I told them to locate my uncle, that I had a dream of him and I didn't like it, but I broke down in the room, because over and over again we see when God speaks to us, shows us through dreams or many different ways of talking to us, and we don't "PRAY FERVENTLY" as we should, I don't blame myself as everyone makes their destiny. But I should have insisted until he had been located or until God had given me rest in my prayer, pray yes!, but it was not a fervent prayer of intercession for him, I should have stayed there, until God had given me peace, In those same days, during the pandemic of death worldwide, Jorge received bad news, that his sister was with COVID-19. From that day on he received that news he prostrated himself before God, making fence, and did not move until he received favorable news from his family in Panama.

Jorge is not perfect, on the contrary, he has many defects, but he does have to know how to lower heaven here on earth. This first month of 2021, the Lord put it in my heart that the church prayed and fasted for 21 days, at 5am, they say that when one sets out to mess with God, the enemy attacks, that is the truth. The second day of prayer was where I received the news of my uncle's death, which by the way hurt me a lot, my grandmother bent so many knees for him, and my mother too, we know by faith God was going to use my uncle strongly, because he was the little sheep that needed God the most in the family.

I prayed with my mother, and we commented that God was going to use him to bring others, and God was going to use him as a powerful testimony for the rest of the family to see his testimony and be converted. On the second day of the 21-day prayer and fasting, I was very hurt by the death of my uncle. I did not tell anyone about that news, since I am very reserved, but in the middle of the prayer, the bishop prays Psalm 46:10, "Be still and know that I am God."

At that very moment I felt strength, if knowing what was happening to me, the Lord told me to be still that I am God, I felt a peace that I cannot explain, my eyes were very heavy from crying so much, but at that moment I felt that I could open my eyes to understand that he is God, and that he has control of all things; Many lost their homes, loved ones, during the pandemic made by the hands of men to control the world.

God's Creation

We all know the story of creation, as introduced to us in the book of Genesis. From the very beginning, we understand that God is our Creator, even if atheists or unbelievers think otherwise. "In the beginning, God created the heavens and the earth" (Genesis 1:1). The book of Genesis is filled with manifestations of God, and I imagine that the devil despises it because it serves as a reminder that he is not the creator of anything—he can only act within the parameters that God allows him. Even in chaos, he has to seek permission from God, or he would have destroyed the entire world by now. In just the first chapter of Genesis, we see God engaging all His senses: "God created," "God moved," "God said," "God saw," "God called," "God formed," and "God blessed" His creation, ensuring that everything would multiply according to its kind, including the sea monsters and the birds of the air. How beautiful is our God! One notable point is when God said, "Let the earth bring forth living creatures after their kind" (Genesis 1:24). While God did create animals, He also commanded the earth to produce living creatures from the dust. When God saw this, He declared it to be good. Furthermore, He said, "Let us create man in our image and likeness, that he may have dominion over the fish of the sea, the birds of the air, the beasts of the field, and every creeping thing." God created man in His own image; male and female, He created them. He also provided every plant and seed for food, indicating that the green plants were for nourishment. I can imagine God observing His creation, much like an artist molding dough into shape with His hands. How beautiful my God is! Genesis 2:7 describes it further: "Then the Lord God formed man from the dust of the ground and breathed into his nostrils the breath of life," as if He were gently blowing life into His creation, and so man became a living being.

The Attempt to Destroy God's Creation

In the state of New Jersey in the United States, a fetus (a baby) has been created by science and was created outside the womb, with devices intended to make humans (babies). That is why during the pandemic they made us go through the nose and throat thing, a test called PCR, that was done to collect our DNA, with our DNA they are creating babies, they use science to see how God has created man; in the laboratories they do tests and examinations with our DNA test of all of us not only to create a bomb that kills everyone in the air, as a tool of mass destruction.

They already created one in Pennsylvania, in the United States, but the baby died a few days after it was created. Because all the devil does is imitate God and wants to be like God, to create; but all he creates is evil. In the end he will be tied up. and he will be thrown into hell with all his minions.

The problem for many murderers on the loose, including doctors and scientists, is that the immune system is free; immunity costs nothing, God gave it to us when we were created, so don't let anyone manipulate you to give you chemicals, including vaccines, made for depopulation and human slaughter. And because I speak like this, "for thou shalt know the truth, and the truth shall set you free," we cannot cover the sun with one finger, we cannot ignore what the devil and his minions have been doing for many years. The devil has been using man and science to destroy God's creation. But I want to make a parenthesis here. "Not all doctors are bad."

My co-worker got some welts on her face, and she doesn't know where they came from. I came across an article from the health department, and reading the week before that, vaccines are doing that, as a side effect. I told the co-worker the truth, that hives in the house are one of the many side effects of vaccines.

It gives me a lot of pain how people are using products made by scientists to put it on the skin, the hair, using the human cells of months-old babies, and they already know that these babies have been killed and exploited by the industry, and they don't care about anything, to say that their face never gets old or the skin.

Between Two Worlds By Elizabeth Walcott

These products are made with human cells from babies; they have extracted these cells from living babies and their organs to create products for the face to remove wrinkles. I don't know about you, but it gives me a pain in my heart how they have exploited human beings and no longer experiment with animals, or plants, but with man, "the image and creation of God."

CHAPTER 8

Two Worlds, Open Your Eyes!

Sadly, *"The New World Order"* is sponsoring fights and confrontations in the crowds, rape, and all kinds of crimes in the streets, and they are paying "righteous for sinners" as the Bible says, who in the last days call bad good and good called evil.

> *20 Woe to those who say good to evil, and evil to good; who make darkness out of light, and darkness light; who put bitter for sweet, and sweet for bitter! (Isaiah 5:20).*

This book is not intended to tell you about the spiritual only, but to open your spiritual eyes and recognize the two worlds in which we are living. The spiritual world and the physical world fight each other. Jesus was accused of something he didn't deserve because he was and is the son of God. However, I want you to understand that in these last days we are living the life of Jesus and the devil's harassment against the church as Jesus did before he was crucified.

God's design to create a world full of Him, the devil is converting it to the design of his kingdom here, because he wants to do the same thing that our God did, create life, but change the nature and design of God. Today there are more satanic churches that worship satan freely, although they have always existed, there has never been as much progress as today.

Satan is creating a world in his own way, where the creation of humans is being procreated in a laboratory, where they are injecting RDNA into vaccines, to change the way we think, act and communicate with God. According to some studies, the vaccine plan was to distance man from God, to create a cold and loveless world.

An atheist scientist gave a talk in 2014, where he explained that they had found a way to penetrate the brain and change what "attracts us to God", make the human being apathetic and less loving to the things of God, that is why many are dying of the heart and you have brain problems, because this atheist scientist supposedly taught the brain and the place where he believes God is.

The Spirit of the Antichrist Is Here

The bioengineer system is modifying the human being, his mind, and the way of thinking, in the physical world, especially in our jobs, the opinion with common sense is already disappearing; we find opinions of others who want to shape our life and the way of living. When a person of gender not acquired by God, he finds that his habit is to manipulate and influence others like the spirit of "Jezebel." The

Bible says that people suffer. "When the righteous rule, the people rejoice; But when the wicked rule, the people groan."

What is bio-engineer? Bio-engineered are processed foods and products made in laboratories; they are not natural. They also have grafted products that alter the DNA of the plants and animals we eat. These chemicals are very harmful to our system, especially our body, such as the liver. These chemicals also produce cancer.

Because I'll explain that, I was sent to military school, and when I was there, I learned a word called "group thinking." Group Thinking in Spanish is "Groupthink." That means that where there is someone who controls and the group you have no opinion and cannot add anything and when you do, that is, when that person says something, "that's it" that person is correct, even if you have a better idea, that person's is the last word and everyone in the group supports him.

We are living in a time where there are people in positions of influence, and no one can tell them anything, because if they don't, they attack you and fall on you. The spirit of the antichrist is dominating the world with satanic people, with weird ideological norms, and the world is supporting them; the church, the government and many more are blind. What about that, that when the antichrist rises up to impose his rules, he will not see anyone who can say "NO." Because even the church is being modified like the bio-engineer."

Modifying pure, holy and healthy things so that the human being is manipulated. When I was praying God reminded me of a movie I saw a long time ago, "Left Behind" referring to the title "The Rapture" along with the word of God that says that in the last times even the elect will be deceived, and I always had a doubt that this would happen "that even the elect will be deceived?"

Now I am living it and seeing it with my own eyes, where the church from the pulpit is preaching love and loving one's neighbor and accepting everyone, excuse me, but the sinner will not enter the kingdom of heaven! The devil's agenda is spreading globally, "equality," I don't know what world they are in! God loves the sinner, but He does not love sin. That's why the Bible says

> *"The soul that sins, that one will die; the Son will not bear the sin of the Father, nor will the Father bear the sin of the Son; the righteousness of the righteous shall be upon him, and the wickedness of the wicked shall be upon him" (Ezekiel 18:20 King James Version 1960, 20).*

This physical and spiritual blindness is due to the lack of prayer and fasting. The Holy Spirit has taught me to pray in a way that I have been asking Him to help me and teach me to pray effectively for this age.

I have been serving the Lord for over 25 years in ministry. And I've learned to depend on the Holy Spirit. Every morning, I pray on the road when I'm driving, and I've always felt the power of the Holy Spirit like I've never felt before. I do it every morning on my way to work in the car. Sometimes, certain mornings I have forgotten to pray, I pray in the early morning as usual, but I did not pray on the way. The demons rise using people around me, that when those attack they arrive, once and for all the Holy Spirit reminds me, the spiritual strategy and prayer is very important.

In the physical (the earth) the enemy uses these people to want to steal our joy. That is why today I want to advise you that, even if you pray at home, the house should not be your only place of altar and prayer. There are people who say I don't feel like praying, oh I don't even feel like praying. Beloved, you will not feel like praying all 365 days of the year, but still submit your flesh to prayer and fasting. *"Pray without ceasing," (1 Thessalonians 5:17).* And you will see the glory of God and the change around you and yours.

In the spiritual world, I am going to translate what you read in the previous paragraph. Satan's kingdom is advancing more than ever.

One morning as I was always praying while I was on my way and I felt a fear like never before, suddenly I felt like someone in a car was shooting me from their window towards mine, while I was driving or like something bad was going to happen to me, I had never felt anything like it in my life, although I have been to places of war like Iraq or other places.

After I felt that fear, in the same week, I went to the bank, and the teller told me that the bank had been robbed. Immediately, the Lord remembered and told me that was what he felt. I always go to that bank about three times a week, but that day I didn't go, I had just returned from Alaska, and I had a lot of work.

Imagine a soldier walking into a bank just as it is being robbed. When God has a purpose for you, no devil or bullet can thwart that purpose. God often reveals His plans to His prophets, warning them of future events. We see this with Abraham in Genesis 18, as well as many others in the scriptures who received advance notice from God about what was to come.

Just think of Noah (Genesis 6), to someone, God is speaking today about what we are going through throughout the earth. When the earth was hit by a demon called COVID, the Holy Spirit once told me,

"Don't inject anything, don't take anything they give you, don't do nose tests, and if you do, clean yourself and don't breathe in that poison, because it's intoxicated."

Unfortunately, many shepherds told their sheep to inject themselves, and many of those sheep have died because of those injections. In my opinion, I believe that many pastors need to repent and ask the people for forgiveness in public for having encouraged the can to inject themselves.

CHAPTER 9

We Are Commanding Generals

A General commands, decrees, cancels, speaks, creates, and approves laws; we, as commanders, act by the command of the Holy Spirit. We were not born by mistake; that is what the devil wanted to insinuate since you were in your mother's womb.

That is why he wanted to kill you, because he knew that if you found your identity in him as a General, you were going to make war on him. As a prophet, I tell you today that you are the voice of God here on earth. We, the Generals' command, have meetings, and we have people under our charge.

Through the Father Yahweh, you are a son or daughter of the King of kings, and as such, you have access to the throne of the eternal God, and as a son or daughter of God, you represent your Father here on earth. There is nothing and no one that can knock you out of His presence, only if you leave your place as a royal priesthood.

What is a General? In earthly forces, it is one of the highest ranks after the president, that is, the commander in control, the one who plans the operation. In this same way, our commander in control and supreme greatest is the trinity, the Father, Son, and the Holy Spirit.

Every General has one to five stars, here on earth. The more that a general does his work and conquers regions, he overthrows enemy kings; conquer regions and nations, the more their chances of promotion.

You don't have to be begging God in prayer. Sometimes we think God is so far away that we expect Him to do everything, but Jehovah is waiting for you to be the one to move to decree in your position as his legitimate son or daughter, in the spirit by adoption. Jesus is the only begotten son, and then we follow.

Let me lay the foundation and the foundation. When in the book of Joshua, in chapters 3, 4, 5:1, the story speaks of the people of Israel conquering the territory that Jehovah had already promised them with Moses; in chapter three Joshua commands the people to follow the Levites where the Ark is, all the tribes lined up, but the first to set foot were those who had the ark, that is, the Levites.

The ark was what represented Jehovah's presence, but before that, Joshua, the commander, directed them by what Jehovah had given them to do. Joshua was called to lead the people, just as Moses had done, but Joshua had to fight in order to take the land.

8 And the children of Israel did it, just as Joshua commanded them: they took twelve stones from the middle of the Jordan, as the Lord had told Joshua, according to the number of the tribes of the children of Israel, and brought them to the place where they camped, and they raised them up there. 9 Joshua also set up twelve stones in the middle of the Jordan, in the place where the feet of the priests who carried the ark of the covenant were. and they have been there until today. 15 Then the LORD spoke to Joshua, saying, 16 Command the priests who carry the ark of the testimony to come up from the Jordan (Joshua 4:8-9; 4:15-16).

When Jehovah gives you a promise, He keeps it. The signs are not only for God's children, but also for the enemy. God reminds us of victories and puts a sign that "If He did it once, He will do it again."

In case you didn't know, you're in training and Father God is training you today!

CHAPTER 10
I'm A Tool In My Father's Hands

Many times, we are so wrong about God. We put Jehovah as a passive and weak God. However, you and I were strategically planned for this time. In case you didn't know, you are a tool of war in the hands of Father God. I'm telling you that I work in the military, when someone creates something, it's because they have a purpose. When we make alliances with countries, it is not only to look cute on social networks, it is to let the enemy know that those who join us, that country is backed by the United States and Europe.

When God created us, he already knew when we were going to fail. Eve and Adam were going to sin, so Jesus came. In Exodus 15:3, it says that the Lord is a man of war, and he uses a man like Moses to shame the most powerful man of war on earth, Pharaoh. There was also another very powerful man in the Bible named Nebuchadnezzar, and after being humbled by God, he recognized that Jehovah is God and there is no other.

In 1 Chronicles 12:22-35, David goes to Ziklag. If you look closely, in this place, Jehovah gave David thousands of men of war, but a man who understood the times, only two hundred. These two hundred were "Chiefs" of the tribe of Issachar, that tribe was very wise, with prophetic direction from the Spirit of God. It means that, although the tribe of Zebulun brought 50,000 experts in troops known in all kinds of tools of war and instruments of war without doubles of heart (i.e., they were ready to disrupt whatever came their way), they submitted to the chiefs.

In other words, though many men of war prepared for any battle—trained men, generals, commanders, in the thousands—the Word says that the brethren, that is, the tribes, followed what the chiefs said. The tribe of Manasseh, which was half of the eighteen thousand tribes, these men was mentioned by name and yet submitted to the voice of the two hundred of the tribe of Issachar. The problem is that many today want others to submit to them, but they don't submit to anyone.

> *32 Of the sons of Issachar, two hundred chiefs who understood the times and knew what Israel should do—all their brethren followed their word. 33 Of Zebulun, fifty thousand seasoned warriors equipped for battle with every kind of weapon, ready to fight with undivided loyalty. 34 Of Naphtali, a thousand captains, and with them thirty-seven thousand men armed with shields and spears (1 Chronicles 12:32-34, NIV). When Saul died, and David was already reigning over Judah in Hebron,*

the other tribes of Israel asked David to be their king. So all the men trained for war went to Hebron with a firm decision to recognize David as king of all Israel. Thus God fulfilled His promise to David (1 Chronicles 11:1-3, NLT). Of the tribe of Judah: six thousand eight hundred armed with shields and spears. Of the tribe of Simeon: seven thousand one hundred mighty soldiers. Of the tribe of Levi: four thousand six hundred. Of the family of Aaron: three thousand seven hundred, with Jehoiada as their leader. Of the family of Zadok, a brave young warrior: twenty-two leaders. Of the tribe of Benjamin, relatives of Saul: three thousand. From the tribe of Ephraim: twenty thousand eight hundred courageous warriors, famous within their clans. Of the half-tribe of Manasseh: eighteen thousand. From the tribe of Issachar: two hundred leaders who understood the times and knew what Israel should do. From the tribe of Zebulun: fifty thousand experienced soldiers ready for battle with all types of weapons. Of the tribe of Naphtali: one thousand captains, and with them thirty-seven thousand men armed with shields and spears. Of the tribe of Dan: twenty-eight thousand six hundred. From the tribe of Asher: forty thousand battle-ready soldiers. From the tribes of Reuben, Gad, and the half-tribe of Manasseh (east of the Jordan): one hundred twenty thousand well-armed soldiers (1 Chronicles 12:24-37, NLT).

The KJV in verse 37 says that they were men, tools, and instruments of war. How can it be possible that if David wasn't their king, then who was he? Saul! If David's men are mentioned in chapter 11, it may be that Jehovah has sent you men to help you in the work, and you have thrown them out and denied ministerial help.

Just as many of us were rejected by pastors, and now Jehovah uses us to be an instrument in his hands, a very special detail that I would like you to learn, the church is not yours, it is My Father's. Don't be easily offended, don't let emotions control your mind and your tongue. This is a war against the Devil and his minions, not of bony flesh with "the human being."

Do this prayer:

Father, I come before You and renounce every spirit of duality and laziness in my life. I uproot every trace of procrastination from my heart. Today, I take control of my physical and spiritual life, submitting myself entirely to the will of the Holy Spirit. I receive the prophetic voice of God and the teachings of the Holy Spirit regarding my life. I am free today from every lie I have heard from false prophets, and I honor the true prophets in the spiritual realm. I acknowledge my calling, and if that is the gift You have given me, I will embrace that calling without reservation. I commit to using it for Christ's kingdom in both the physical and spiritual worlds. I walk in my role as a prophet; this is my identity! I am an instrument of war in my Father's hands. I will not entertain a double-minded spirit. I cast it out now and forever.

Between Two Worlds By Elizabeth Walcott

The War Between the Two Worlds

I fight physical warfare, since that is my job, but spiritual warfare, thank God, I do not see it with my physical eyes, but I have experienced it. As I told you earlier, about my experience when I was driving, and praying in tongues. When I'm handling, I pray in tongues, and I get into the depths. Just like it happened to me, while I was praying in my car, as always, I felt a horrible oppression, I felt like when you have criminals next to you, I felt afraid as if someone was going to shoot me, and I would have to defend myself, not only the military antennas that I already have because of my training were put on alert, but also spiritual ones.

In the same way as Generals of the living God, we are always alert in the prophetic area. Let us be on the alert, so brethren, I do not want you to be ignorant. Generals plan strategically to attack the enemy; you don't have to sweat in the fight. You have to be filled with the Holy Spirit and His Word so that you can use the right tools to destroy the enemy and his followers. Satan's kingdom has already been destroyed. if you don't believe me, read the book of Revelation.

The week of Azuza was celebrated at River City Church, here in Illinois. Apostle Dutch Sheets came and prophesied a word for this time. I had already returned from DC a week before, when I was in Washington, DC for work reasons, not knowing that I was going to Washington, DC that week. God immediately showed me that I had to decree a few words about Washington, DC.

In the early hours of Friday morning in DC to leave for Illinois, God told me I want you to go running in the streets, instead of being in the car, this time you are going to run and in what you run I want you to pray and intercede for the capital of the United States Washington DC. When I was on my knees, I felt how the Holy Spirit showed me how interceding that prayer was something like this;

Father, I want that when I run, in the streets, your presence will be manifested here in the state of Washington, that when I set my feet in the streets, it will be you, tearing down everything that does not please you, and all the work of the enemy is under the feet of your children here in this place, use me as an instrument here that your glory and your power will be notorious in the presidential White House. in the government here as the capital of the United States. That each law aligns with yours; Use every representative here, Lord in the White House, I'm a representative of your glory and your government here on earth.

I felt God's presence go with me as I ran through the streets of Washington, D.C., God prepared me in Azuza through the impartation of His Word for when I was there in Washington. Upon returning to the hotel, I felt in my soul a great weight and desire to cry, for this state, God told me, I have placed that burden on you to intercede for Washington DC greater now that you have stepped on earth and I have taught you the need to intensify your prayer for Washington.

I want to add that Satanists and sorcerers do the same thing, they pray for Washington, but in a contrary way, so that Washington

DC will fall and the works and kingdom of satan will prevail there in the Capital of Washington DC.

In case you didn't know, you are one of the most powerful tools of war that has ever existed here on earth, the devil is afraid of you. But it's when you understand that you're not you, you're the most powerful thing that Jesus left here on earth, it's Jesus himself still walking on earth inside you, an instrument worse than an atomic bomb. That is why Paul said, "I do not live but Christ lives in me."

If you knew who you were, you would not fight with mosquitoes or insects or snakes, but you would strike down giants daily, like those men of David. Because before we were warning against physical enemies, but today we are warring with spiritual enemies, demons, hosts of evil.

The Voice of God

When we don't pay attention to God's voice and the church is dwarfed, people don't grow, the devil takes over that church, and keeps it monotonous. Cold worship services and it becomes a routine, nothing more, that's why many stay at home and watch from the internet, because they already know that the church is going to conduct routine worship, "every day" is the same thing.

The same songs, the same people—Pastor, let the presence of God immerse your church. Allow the Holy Spirit to take over the worship and the congregation. When Saul fell and the presence of God departed from him, it was because he did not obey God's voice; His presence was no longer with him. David was chosen by God, while Saul was chosen by the people. Saul was rejected by the Lord because he stopped listening to God's voice, resulting in the absence of God's presence in his life, unlike that of David and Moses. *"If your presence does not go with us, do not take us up from here." (Exodus 33:15).* Even if the enemy hears what God is planning for your life, do not be afraid. Threats will come from the enemy; for example, Jezebel heard what Elijah had done. However, what she did not realize was that it was God who used Elijah to glorify His name. Although what God achieved through Elijah posed a threat to her Baals—her pagan and strange gods—it was ultimately a demonstration of God's power.

On the other hand, abandonment occurs when someone is evicted or separated from us; that is, they move away so as not to have responsibility for us. Organizations break away, governments break away, and abandon their responsibilities and coverage. Fathers abandon their children and wives because they don't want responsibility; they don't want to carry that responsibility.

So many times we feel abandoned in ministry, especially when we have someone to do what God has commanded, many men and women of God feel alone, and abandonment causes emotional pain and confusion. Abandonment can be physical, emotional and psychological, when a baby does not feel the fondness of their parents, they cling to the extreme or to something else, for example, their partners or work, because they know that is all they have.

When that fails them, they even want to take their own lives on many occasions, since they clung to what their eyes see, since the spiritual is not seen, they do not want to put their trust in what is not seen. There are Christians who have regressed and waned in seeking and praying because they feel burdened and heavy with the ministry burden. I want to speak to you on this day of the abandonment that many have had either by their parents, brethren in the church, and even pastors who promised many that they were going to be there and never came.

When we examine Paul's life during his imprisonment, particularly in 2 Timothy 4:11-21, we see him expressing a desire for the physical companionship of those who had accompanied him in ministry. In verse 10, Paul notes that Demas has abandoned him to pursue worldly interests, while Titus is in Dalmatia. Interestingly, in Colossians, Demas and Luke are mentioned together in ministry, with Luke being recognized as the beloved physician.

When someone follows the guidance of the Holy Spirit, they often let go of attachments to the world. While many choose to serve God instead of pursuing worldly desires, they also find friends who can facilitate connections between different ministries and support one another. However, when a person feels abandoned, it can lead to a loss of trust. This is why many individuals struggle to believe in or help others; they may lack faith or trust in those around them.

It is sad to see how Christians are afraid to help someone for fear of being betrayed or abandoned in ministry. Relationships in the pulpit have broken down due to a lack of belief and faith in the person; distrust is an indication that you have not matured for God to use the members of the church.

Now we have to put a pause here, we know that our fight is not against flesh, that means that before putting someone in the pulpit, you must first have the spirit of discernment, you cannot put or believe in anyone if it has not been confirmed by the Holy Spirit. Not everyone wants good in your ministry, not everyone wants to help you, many come to know what God is doing in you, and then wish you evil in your ministry.

Therefore, you must test the spirits and see if they are of God or followers of the devil. Paul talked a lot about his disciples, Timothy, Mark, Tychicus, Gaius, Sopater, and Titus (Titus 1:4 KJV). These men and many others were with Paul for a long time; together they went to Greece and Macedonia.

Pablo hugged them, kissed them, shared with them, and had a very beautiful friendship of brotherhood. Paul stayed with Luke and asked Mark to come to him, who is useful to him for the ministry. How is it that Paul is so close to the Apostles and disciples? Because he knew how to put his emotions and although he was alone in prison, he never stopped writing and communicating with them. My question today is, who are you positively influencing?

Being filled with His Glory makes us immovable in the face of the enemy. God did not forget us.

God is aligning His church, awakening a powerful movement that will encompass every atmospheric zone, where the enemy will not be able to operate in the minds of the unbelievers anymore, because the signs will be notorious, massive healings, liberation and renewal of forces will manifest on the face of the earth; territories and governments are going to fall under the mighty hand of Jehovah.

We are surrounded by a glory that, although we do not see it, the Holy Spirit is sending his angels to you; the angels are fighting for you, for your children, and for your house. That is why we need to maintain a life of prayer to call those angels to war for us as we continue to pray and fast. Daniel's story is well known to everyone, but Daniel fought in the spirit and in the physical; your enemies are more spiritual than physical.

Earthly influences are a result of you getting closer to your purpose, and that is why it is the fight against you, in your work, sudden illnesses, divorces, and abuse. That's precisely because the enemy wants to neglect you and keep you distracted from God's plan for you.

No one can fight for you like you yourself, under the power of the Holy Spirit. Use the gifts and ask the Holy Spirit to show you the areas you have to fight internally so that, spiritually, you are trained.

CHAPTER 11

When The Devil Takes Away What You Love Most

Virginia is my friend and spiritual sister who serves in all the regions of Panama. Her testimony reads as follows: "My daughter left a letter before she left with the Lord. When my daughter left with the Lord, I had a word. "The ways of the Lord. Mom, the best thing that has happened to us is to know Jesus. Do not be dismayed, forgive all my faults. Go on."

I had a very great pain, I began to cry, and I told the Lord, I stay with you. When you meet Jesus, many things stop mattering to you, your priorities change, and your total surrender and love for God is infinite.

You can already smell victory!

One early morning, being in California, I had never been to California, the Lord said to me, Do you smell victory? My King Jesus is an expert in victories, the one who has not lost any of the wars, says to you today, Do you smell your victory? From level to level, God prepares us, both physically and spiritually.

It's almost time to go to Africa, the group of intercessors was praying on Zoom, and when I finished being in my room, the Lord told me do you smell victory? The Lord gave us instructions to do before going to Africa, one of them was not to worry that He is with us, to pray more in the spirit, and third to anoint our eyes with anointed oil, and finally, to blow the shofar before praying every day.

The eye is the lamp of the body. Therefore, if your vision is clear, your whole being will enjoy the light, (Matthew 6:22, NIV). Through the eyes the enemy can enter; if you don't believe me, ask Eva. In the eyes there is light as darkness; the children of the living God walk in light, but those of darkness walk in darkness. The anointing of God at the moment of distributing something that comes from Him, if we are very focused on the things around, easily the word that is going to be given is prostituted, but when our eyes are covered and sealed, the enemy cannot penetrate our spirit.

Many times we as children of light do not know why many preachers, especially prophets, and those who have been called to the Apostolic anointing work on a different level and many times we do not understand what they do. Before giving the word, they remain in their prayer room and go out to the last of the praises, it is not because we do not want to be praising God with you together.

But God Himself has us in a place that I call "virgin" in that place where there is no penetration or conflict of Christology. When I was sleeping I felt like the Lord was telling me that the enemy is preparing and attacking and that we have to get up. I immediately got up praying in tongues, and connected with the intercessors of Massachusetts. Pray in tongues I told them, and immediately we began to pray in tongues. Pastor Edna received confirmation to anoint our eyes. Finally, the Shofar, the shofar has many prophetic meanings that means prepare for war, it reminds us that Jehovah is our King.

On a war footing

David came from one war and entered another without knowing what awaited him. God's mantle is upon you. In the book of Colossians he says,

> *"And stripping (disarming) principalities and powers, he exhibited them publicly, triumphing over them on the cross," (Colossians 2; 15).*

The enemy was stripped of something that did not belong to him, it is when someone seizes something that is not theirs. Paul in the book of Colossians reminds them that the customs or rites of the Jews are already under the dominion and power of the cross, that being in Christ those rites are only symbolic.

The Gentiles are in Christ, and they don't need to do that anymore. God's command is upon us, when we are in him, that the enemy (satan) has been disarmed, destitute, deprived of everything that did not belong to him, Jesus disarmed him, defeated him, expelled him, and took away from him all the dominion that Adam and Eve had granted him for having sinned in Eden.

In the military, when an enemy is disarmed and expelled from what he had, he is useless, he is a slave of the new owner, he has no way to defend himself, how to win the battle, he has already lost it, he has no way to fight. That is why it is very important that we do not give room to the enemy, because otherwise, we are going to be the ones who are unarmed and defeated.

The one who hates you, desires your death, and pushes you violently into the Kingdom of God, that is Satan.

However, enemies come to give you more tools, the purpose of which is to draw you closer to your purpose and calling. The purpose is to prepare you for the coming war, which, even if you don't see it, is preparing you for a victory beforehand. Enemies come to help you get closer to God.

The enemies come to train you to reach the highest level, It's like a pressure cooker, the more fire you put on it, the stronger the pressure, you can't uncover that pot, because if you uncover it by the pressure the lid will go to the ceiling. Likewise, when God passes you through the fire, the more fire there is, the higher the pressure there is. David, having just come from one war, entered another without knowing what awaited him.

Between Two Worlds By Elizabeth Walcott

David and his men arrived at Ziglag on the third day. Now the Amalekites had raided the Negev and Ziklag. They had attacked Ziklag and burned it, 2 and had taken captive the women and all who were in it, young and old. They did not kill any of them, but took them away as they went. 3 When David and his men arrived at Ziklag, they found it destroyed by fire, and their wives and sons and daughters had been taken captive. 4 Then David and his men wept aloud until they had no strength left to weep. 5 David's two wives had been captured: Ahinoam of Jezreel and Abigail, widow of Nabal of Carmel. 6 David was greatly afflicted because the men were talking about stoning him. Each one was bitter in spirit because of his sons and daughters. But David found strength in the Lord his God. 7 Then David said to Abiathar the priest son of Ahimelech, "Bring me the ephod." Abiathar brought it to him, (1 Samuel 30:1-7).

Everything is lawful for me, but not everything builds up. We see how the world and the church are being polluted; everything is lawful for me, but not everything is good for me. There is a force moved by cultural influence, where it seems to be God, but it is not God. There is no holiness; the things of the world are lawful for me, but it does not edify my spirit, and it do not bring honor to God.

When the church and the world excuse sin, that's when the spirit of the antichrist comes in. In recent times, apostasy has crept into the church; what seems to be of God is not. When humanity does not know how to distinguish between sin and holiness, it has lost the narrow gate and the narrow way. The wide road and gate is what many are preferring today.

> *"Enter through the narrow gate; for wide is the gate, and broad is the way that leads to destruction, and many there are that enter through it." (Matthew 7:13-14)*

The church is holy because God is holy. God loves the sinner, but He does not love sin.

CHAPTER 12
Jehovah's Kingdom Vs. Satan's

David, a warrior of God, knew how to face physical and spiritual enemies. In the book of Proverbs 18:10, when we study the word "Tower" means in Hebrew Mildal, something tall that is made of many stones, and is built for military purposes of strategies, which are located in strategic places for battle in order to use them as a defensive part of the city.

Three things I can see as welded. 1st. High made of fortified stones all around. 2nd. Built for military purposes. 3rd. Located in strategic places. You can imagine Father Jehovah acting like this on our behalf. Wherever the enemy dares to mess with one of his children, My Father is like a strong tower, rather he is a strong tower around us, paralyzing and crumbling every argument and every tool of the enemy that wants to come against us.

And this tower that I described to you is earthly the more so the one that My Father has put around us. On the top of the third heaven is your tower; Built for protection purposes and at the same time located in your home, at work, around you and wherever you and yours go.

> "The name of the Lord is a strong tower; To him shall the righteous run, and he shall be lifted up" (Proverbs 18:10).

If we look at the books of Proverbs and Psalms we find a link in this chapter 18 of the book of Proverbs. Reading the previous verses it seems that they have nothing to do with each other, but they do have a lot to do with it. The haughty, bad, despotic man does not understand the things of God, here is a stop in verses 1 to 9, he only speaks of someone who is arrogant and evil.

The righteous must know that God is their protector and caretaker, when the one who persecutes you is despotic, evil, does not understand the things of God. But you and I are protected by Jehovah. Proverbs 18:1-9 speaks of someone who is your enemy, but in verse 10, it speaks of divine protection.

Let the wicked one talk all he wants, in the end they will not be able to beat you, their spears and tools will not be able to defeat you, since Jehovah is your strong tower.

> *For the weapons of our warfare are not carnal, but mighty in God for the breaking down of strongholds, 5 casting down arguments and every lofty thing that exalts itself against the knowledge of God, and bringing every thought captive to the obedience of Christ, 6 and being ready to punish all*

disobedience, when your obedience is perfect" (2 Corinthians 10:4-6 KJV).

David said in one of the Psalms,

"For you have been my refuge and a strong tower from the enemy" (Psalm 61:3).

I also advise you to read Judges chapter 9. Abimelech kills 70 brothers; he also destroys and kills many soldiers. Abimelech was a strong soldier like David, with strategies, the only thing that was the opposite of David. Abimelech was evil and had many soldiers like him, wicked men whom he trained. Although the governor was on Abimelech's side, in Judges 9 it says that he confronted Gaal and his brothers and could not beat Abimelech. Abimelech went to Thebes where he fought there also. But...

52 And Abimelech came to the tower, and fighting it, he came to the gate of the tower to set it on fire. 53 But a woman dropped a piece of a millstone on Abimelech's head, and broke his skull, (Joshua 9:52).

A woman... filled with the wisdom of God, in this high tower, where they were all hiding from Abimelech, she was able to use the wisdom that comes from Jehovah. Thousands of people took refuge in that tower, but there was one brave woman who did not care about her threats, nor about Abimelech's reputation.

She took courage and even though she didn't have a physical sword she used what she found, so we have to be in the things of Jehovah. To be hidden in the tower that is Christ, and at the same time to use the tools that God has given us.

Don't be afraid to face the enemy, and put a stop to him, because if not, he will try to continue killing and destroying your house, your life and your city. God is looking for brave people who will stand up and stand in the war to intercede and act against the enemy. From the tower, soldiers position themselves with tools to see and be able to kill and destroy the enemy.

God has put us on high, where we are seated together with Christ. Be like the eagle that walks in the heights and looks down to get its prey.

> *6 He raised us up with him, and also made us sit in the heavenly places with Christ Jesus, 7 to show in the ages to come the abundant riches of his grace in his kindness to us in Christ Jesus (Ephesians 2:6-7).*

In heavenly places there is authority, power and dominion, do not walk with your head down, Jesus did not make such a great sacrifice for us so that we would walk from defeat to defeat, but His sacrifice was for you to represent Him here on earth.

In other words, so that his kingdom may be every day, taking and having possession here on earth, to destroy the enemy, to shame satan and his demons. Paul, in the book of Colossians, chapter 2:10, 14-15 says,

> *And ye are complete in Him, who is the head of all principality and power. This includes every principality, every demon, and every host of wickedness operating in the heavenly realms."*

Where Speak goes on and says,

> *14 He annulled the record of the decrees that were against us, which was contrary to us, and put it out of the way by nailing it to the cross. 15 And he despoiled the principalities and the authorities and exhibited them publicly, triumphing over them on the cross.*

The Baraca Valley 1 Chronicles 20

"Elhanan" is a boy's name of Hebrew origin. It comes from the Hebrew word *"elchanan,"* which means *"to whom God gave."* Other interpretations of the name include *"grace of God"* and *"to whom God has graciously granted."* In the Hebrew Bible, Elhanan is depicted as a great warrior in David's army, known for having killed Goliath's brother. Elhanan is the son of Jair, a name that also has Hebrew origins, meaning *"He will illuminate."* This could be interpreted as *"The Enlightened One," "Illuminated by God," "Yahweh illuminates,"* or *"God wants to shine."*

God wants to shine in your children, just as he has given you victories in your life, there comes a great fire from the movement of the Holy Spirit, where what God has given you by grace, your children will receive double. That's why you have to fight for them, fight for them, get into your bedroom right now and start feeling how the power of God covers you as you read this book, because God says to you today,

> *"Fight for yours, and don't let go, because I'm going to use you and your descendants, since the enemy is behind them. But he will not be able to bear your descendants, for I have given you grace before me, and your children will possess more than I have given you. My light is upon them, to war and destroy the giants with whom they are confronting. Those Goliaths are going to fall and will be destroyed by my hand," says the Lord Jehovah of hosts, the great and fearful. War in the Spirit, that I'm already positioning them for many victories. "I" have enlightened them and chosen them for this time, to bring down the heads of giants, to plant and destroy kingdoms.*

> *In the spring, at the time when kings go off to war, Joab led out the armed forces. He laid waste the land of the Ammonites and went to Rabbah and besieged it, but David remained in Jerusalem. Joab attacked Rabbah and left it in ruins. ² David took the crown from the head of their king[a]—its weight was found to be a talent[b] of gold, and it was set with precious stones—and it was placed on David's head. He took a great quantity of plunder from the city ³ and brought out the*

people who were there, consigning them to labor with saws and with iron picks and axes. David did this to all the Ammonite towns. Then David and his entire army returned to Jerusalem. (1 Chronicles 20:1-3)

Warriors

Who better to talk to you about war than a warrior in the American Army who has been trained to do many things and defend the nation? However, this war is not carnal, but spiritual; the enemy does not walk around with silly tools and trifles. He walks around with the most powerful tools that you can think of "yourself", the atomic bombs do not even reach his ankles. For what he has prepared for all of us, he is only interested in souls going to hell.

⁴ The weapons we fight with are not the weapons of the world. On the contrary, they have divine power to demolish strongholds. ⁵ We demolish arguments and every pretension that sets itself up against the knowledge of God, and we take captive every thought to make it obedient to Christ. ⁶ And we will be ready to punish every act of disobedience, once your obedience is complete. (2 Corinthians 10:4-6)

The enemy wants to destroy your home, your businesses, your ministries, and any other area he can destroy, if you make room for him, or someone in your house has given it to him. If this is the case for you, repeat this prayer out loud with me.

Prayer: Every strategy of the devil and his demons even people who have used as his followers, I come in the mighty name of Jesus of Nazareth, tearing down every argument that was raised or is raised against me in this day, and in days to come, and bring it subject and captive to the obedience of Christ. Every contrary spirit in this hour I rebuke and bind in the name of Jesus, and throw him out into the dry place from which he came, either by satanic prayers made against the church that I am. Or through objects, photos, all activity of satanic rites and prayers against me and the church at this time is inoperative in the name of Jesus, almighty. I unite worldwide with all of Christ's intercessors under this prophetic office and mantle, and declare the word that says in the book of Matthew 18:19, "Again I say to you, if two of you agree on earth about anything they ask, it will be done for them by my Father who is in heaven. 20 For where two or three are gathered together in my name, there am I in the midst of them." In this covenant and in agreement I join with my brethren and declare that it is done. Father, Thy will be done here on earth as it is in heaven.

Remember your calling

The words of your mouth have power (1 Kings 17:24). When the enemy comes against you and yours: You need to know who it is that called you.

[14] And Hezekiah received the letter from the hand of the messengers, and read it: and Hezekiah went up unto the house

of the Lord, and spread it before the Lord. [15] And Hezekiah prayed unto the Lord, saying, [16] O Lord of hosts, God of Israel, that dwellest between the cherubims, thou art the God, even thou alone, of all the kingdoms of the earth: thou hast made heaven and earth. [17] Incline thine ear, O Lord, and hear; open thine eyes, O Lord, and see: and hear all the words of Sennacherib, which hath sent to reproach the living God. [18] Of a truth, Lord, the kings of Assyria have laid waste all the nations, and their countries, [19] And have cast their gods into the fire: for they were no gods, but the work of men's hands, wood and stone: therefore they have destroyed them. [20] Now therefore, O Lord our God, save us from his hand, that all the kingdoms of the earth may know that thou art the Lord, even thou only. (Isaiah 37:14-20 KJV).

Practically Hezekiah said to God, Look! "They have made war on us." War has existed before the foundation of the world, from the Garden of Eden with Adam and Eve, to the call of the Gentiles to be converted to Christ. It seems that we enlist in the army at birth, without having signed a contract in the earthly army.

I know I signed a contract with the army, but I didn't realize it when I signed the spiritual one. I think that in order to answer my own question, it was at the moment of birth. That's why the devil is attacking children from the womb, to kill them, because he knows that if that baby is born, it immediately becomes a threat to him.

Just that possibility that that baby will be operating in one or more of the five ministries of the church is already a danger to him. So Hezekiah put the problem before God, "the cards on the table," and worshipped. Those who fell before the Assyrians were because they were not real God, they were made of wood and statues made by the hands of men; our God is not made with the hands of men, he dwells among cherubim, he created everything that is seen and exists.

> *22 He sits on the circle of the earth, whose inhabitants are like locusts; He stretches out the heavens like a curtain, spreads them out like a tent to dwell in, (Isaiah 40:22).*

I believe in Jehovah... I believe in His power!

There is no one like him, nor will there be, even if they want to imitate Jehovah, they will not be able to, because He is unique and true, consuming fire, we are like locusts, he sits in the circle of the earth, power and glory is his.

> *[28] But I know thy abode, and thy going out, and thy coming in, and thy rage against me. [29] Because thy rage against me, and thy tumult, is come up into mine ears, therefore will I put my hook in thy nose, and my bridle in thy lips, and I will turn thee back by the way by which thou camest. (Isaiah 37:28-29).*

King Hezekiah has the prophet Isaiah on his side, next to him to give him a word of encouragement. The prophet speaks on behalf of God, and Isaiah speaks on behalf of Jehovah to Hezekiah. In verses 28-29, the Lord stands before King Hezekiah and tells him that the king of Assyria, Sennacherib, has gone against the Lord because the Lord has seen his arrogance.

When someone messes with God's children, they are interfering with Father God Himself. My Father God, Jehovah, doesn't often speak about acting directly! Those who oppose us are often unaware of the source of their downfall, which comes suddenly, like withered grass; thus, Jehovah removes them from this land. Just as our enemies approach us in one way, they will flee in seven.

The worst thing someone in a position of authority can do is forget that all souls belong to Christ, including those labeled as ministerial. A piece of advice I feel led to share today is: do not close the door on anyone; you never know how God might work through that person in your ministry. However, it is also important to discern who is truly with you and who is against you.

Always strive to maintain peace with everyone. Don't exclude anyone from your community; if you fail to reach out, you're misstepping as a leader. Your position does not grant you the authority to obstruct what God is doing in someone's life.

CHAPTER 13
Father

Every time I say, Father, I feel a sound come out of my mouth that sounds like a trumpet. Every time I say "Father" I feel the walls shake, especially when I'm worshiping Him and speaking in the Spirit. *"The demons believe and tremble"* (James 2:19) at the mention of his name, the power to call and cry out to Jehovah is known here on earth, "Cry to me and I will answer you" that is a promise, call him... and you will see how the situation changes or if not, fast, pray, do sackcloth. We are His children; you are His daughter and son.

Do not be afraid of anything; your heavenly Father is with you, waiting for you to cry out to Him. There is a power in crying out and in mentioning his name. Take a few minutes and tell him... Father! Jehovah needed you more than ever. We are his children, not slaves, because the slave has no right to the inheritance, but we do. The angels cannot identify with that word, but you and I can, our Father who art in heaven.

Worship Him that you have a Father who is attentive to your prayer, when you call Him, everything that is next to you or in front of you whether spiritual or physical, has to move and get out of your way, because one of His children is calling the Father. I felt a unique power of authority, as if I was immediately in the presence of something so powerful and magnificent and supreme before me, I felt its protection, and dare I say that the Father is attentive when we call upon Him. God is Omnipotent, Omniscient, He is everywhere, and He is the only one who can be everywhere at the same time; there is no other.

"My son, I am here listening to you, I am the onewho opens doors, and no one can close, I am the one who closes it, and no one can open it."

God's Will Never Fails

My God never fails, never... never... I saw the Lord, and He heard my cry and answered me. He never fails, I believe God, I don't walk by what I see and hear, but by faith and what Jehovah has said about me. My mother used to tell me when I was little, "You're stubborn." Since I was a child I was in the ways of the Lord, my neighbor was an Adventist pastor, my family on my father's side is Adventist.

I had a grandmother who believed in God and prayed a lot for her children. my father was the oldest of all her children. I believe that the inheritance of the firstborn is positioned in me. My father was the firstborn; he had many blessings, but his firstborn daughter, "I," has inherited the inheritance in Christ Jesus. I believe that there is a great blessing when grandparents, parents and Christian ancestors pray for their children and grandchildren; those blessings are passed on to the children, grandchildren, great-grandchildren, etc.

> *"Speak unto all the congregation of the children of Israel, and say unto them, Thou shalt be holy: for I am holy the Lord your God" (Leviticus 19:2).*

The spirit of the antichrist is already at work here on earth, and it is within the churches, with false doctrines, imitating the power of God and deceiving many, even the elect. God is merciful, and His love will reach many, especially those who truly desire His presence.

But at the same time, the devil is deceiving many, churches jumping and jumping, but without power, only screams. It doesn't fit in my head nor will I "NEVER" be able to understand the mixture of the secular with the holy and pure of God. When I say secular, I mean world music, dances, coordinated jumps as if they were in a discotheque.

Nor will I understand what worship and praise have to do with puppets and masks painted white in church. When I see that, I get a zeal for God's house! They are enveloping young people and dancing to music created and inspired by the children of the devil. "The truth will set you free." The father of lies is Satan, and in him there is no truth, there is no light. Jesus clearly said that light has to do with darkness.

44 You are of your father the devil, and you will do your father's desires. He has been a murderer from the beginning, and has not abided in the truth, because there is no truth in him. When he speaks a lie, he speaks of himself; for he is a liar, and the father of lies, (John 8:44).

In the preceding verses, Jesus spoke to them as truly were His disciples; He also told them that if the Son delivers you, you will be free indeed. Jesus reminds them that if they are truly children of Abraham, why do they not understand his words, and why do they seek to kill me? They could not understand the language of Jesus, and they sought to kill him, because they were and are children of the devil.

It sounds strong, but it's the truth, Jesus said your Father's desires you want to do. And I ask you what Satan's desire was in that hour? Exactly, to kill Jesus! And to destroy God's creation, to stop the sacrifice of the Cross and not be redeemed by the blood of the Lamb that is Jesus.

These secular music singers live a life in sin, drink, take drugs, go about fornication and adultery; And you think that the church that's supposed to be holy as God is holy, can be singing and dancing that music? I don't think so, the Holy Spirit has given me conviction that my God is Holy, and I must maintain a holy life as He is.

The Attack on Your Character

Soldiers study enemies, we study them in the areas: Air, sea, interethnic, space, cybernetics, earthly and many more. To counter attack the enemy you have to have mental agility, a strong mind, not a lazy mind, the lazy mind does not get anywhere, the enemy has taken a lot of territory, he attacks you and if you do not attack him he gets stronger, how long are we going to continue ignoring the attacks of the devil and his followers?

There are people who say, "I don't mess with the devil!" But if you don't have to mess with him, the enemy is going to get in and fight against you. You don't have to deliberately attack every day, what I mean is that you have to stand up and at war.

If Jesus was attacked all the time, why do we believe that Satan is not going to mess with us, the children of God? I want to remind you of the story of Job, let's see, did Job mess with the devil? If only because he was righteous, the devil messed with Job, only because he was upright, God-fearing and upright, (Job 1:2). No war is won with arms crossed.

In the Old Testament, none of the battles were won by sitting idly by. That is why I will never understand those who want victory, but do not pray, fast, or do sackcloth or vigil in the presence of God. They don't go to the mountain as Jesus did (in your separate room for God). The problem is that if satan doesn't mess with you, it's because you're not counteracting the devil's kingdom.

Perhaps you are very passive (God do this, or that, fight for me!) No way! Wars are not won like that. The kingdom of heaven suffers violence, and only the brave take it.

In this chapter, you will learn what many do not know, when we face the enemy. In fact, your mouth not only has power when you use the word of God, but when you use the right words and your life filled with the power of God and in every situation, you are still creating and writing the chapters here on earth as in the spiritual world, it is manifested here on earth, with all that you say.

The enemy wants to destroy your character, your integrity, to accuse you before God and say that you are worthless and that you are not His child. When a nation is against another nation (at war) here on earth, the goal of each nation is to destroy the character and disarm that nation, so that other peoples will see what I have done to that nation, and that the same thing I did to this nation, I will do to you as well.

The enemy wants to make people think that you have no value, that you have no integrity, that your actions are questionable, creating lies so that others see you below so that when you want to do something for God, the church, and your family do not believe in you, so that you see yourself and feel defeated. Remember Elijah, after Jehovah glorified himself with the Baals, Jezebel declared war on Elijah.

But in this very hour, arise in the Name of Jesus, and take your stand as a child of God, and do not be intimidated by the enemy. Read and proclaim aloud the Psalm (144:5-8).

Prayer: Deliver me from any vindication to show the people around me that I am free from any doubt or guilt. And that every lying tongue is now silent in the name of Jesus. I oppose any falsehood, slander, speculation, accusations, and misrepresentations and negative character evaluations against me, in the mighty name of Jesus.

Pray for God's Divine Justice, for it is just and if we earnestly seek Him He hears us, He will throw lightning bolts to disperse His accuser, He sent His hand from above and to deliver you from them, To forbid the accusations of the brethren to operate or influence the soul or mind of anyone who comes into contact with Me.

Prayer: I declare and decree that my name is associated with integrity, holiness, justice, and nobility, and that God will vindicate me, I forbid the enemy to advance against my integrity, health, and testimony. Today he tied him up and threw him into the dry place, where his works against me are inoperative. In Jesus' name, Amen.

Remember that the enemy is persistent, so you must be persistent in prayer and intercession in tongues.

CHAPTER 14
Regional Intercession

Our nations need God like never before. The need to pray to God more than ever in history is today. There has always been reason to pray, but today we see how the enemy has risen up against God's church and creation, including our natural land that saw us grow. Crying out to the one true God is our most powerful tool. In the right atmosphere the Apostles, prophets and intercessors being united in one Spirit, "The Holy Spirit" God will confirm what He is doing and speaking at this time.

Pastor Harrigan said that the Kansas team was going to win the 2024 Super American Football Finals. And so it was, that same week in a parade for success, there was a parade for having won the Super Bowl, many people went to celebrate, but tragically the enemy used someone to cause chaos, unfortunately between bullets and deaths the parade ended.

When there is victory, many times the enemy brings havoc and sadness, because he wants to take away the joy of the human being. This region of Kansas is blessed by God, because there is a people praying a lot for this region. God showed me that the local churches need to be united in order to attack the principalities and hosts of evil that operate in the atmosphere of each region.

When a church has a vision limited to just its congregation, it loses a lot in the spiritual environment and does not understand the Kingdom assignment. Pastor Harrigan has a broader vision than many I have heard. The expansion of the church needs the support of everyone in order to achieve a more strategic reach of souls, no army wins only with a single company or unit, the enemy is attacked according to its size, the pastor said at the beginning of the year that the principalities have moved to the region that he is. The enemy and his arsenals are well organized, they know us, they move places when the principalities give their authorization, and that is when the churches are not united in interceding.

Because if the local churches were united, the enemy will not be able to wreak havoc, because he knows that he cannot get into that region. A pastor shared with me that a witch doctor appeared to him and threatened him not to worship further. So what do we do, do we go backwards? No, we cannot turn back from our place of war, since, as ambassadors of Christ, we have legality and dominion in this world. The enemy is forbidden in prayer that he may trespass into the places.

Between Two Worlds By Elizabeth Walcott

"Every place that treads on the sole of your foot shall be yours," Deuteronomy 11:24.

The earth was created for us, not for the kingdom of satan and his demons; His place is hell, which was prepared for him and those who follow him. Therefore, you bring blessings and dislodge everything that does not want to submit to the light.

My children, you bring my blessings, you are sealed with my blessings, when someone approaches you, it is because I want to free them, they come to you so that you can bless them away from the evil one, since the evil one curses them. People who don't have my blessings walk in darkness, because one of my blessings is to be in the light. Attn: you heavenly Father, (Luke 6:22).

In this paragraph, God told me to write it, for you specifically, in what you read this book. One very early morning, I had a dream and saw a man cursed by the enemy coming towards me and everyone in that house.

I tell you and explain the dream: It was like walking in autumn time, and while I was in a house, like in a forest, and with guests, while we were cleaning the kitchen, I observed a person in dark clothes, but I could not see his face, from inside you could only see his shadow reflected through the window. After finishing, all the guests came out, I was the last one, and the owners of the house were ahead of me. I noticed that he was arguing with his wife, but we kept walking, and everything was normal. Suddenly, I saw how the earth opened up and something pulled her by the feet, and although her husband wanted to help her, he couldn't, and suddenly he took him too. That dark shadow took them both, but as it came toward me, I said, "I bind you and rebuke you in Jesus' name." Immediately his face was uncovered, and in his appearance I could see what he looked like, an old white man about very old, with a beard, and the shadow of a whirlwind went away, but the man said to me, 'Bless me!' And the shadow took him again, it was dark, and I said, I bless you in Jesus' name, I could immediately see his face again, he was an old man, and he wanted to be free.

I woke up in the middle of the dream, and I asked God to tell me what this dream meant. Let's pause, and I want to explain what I've been facing in my work. I am going to break down the attacks and discrimination that many of the soldiers unfortunately go through in the Military Forces. When the light is in one place, the darkness cannot do what it wants. For darkness to do anything, they have to take out the light and turn it off, trying to destroy the character and integrity of a Christian; it is one of satan's tools. Since he can't do more than four things, he uses the people around you to destroy you, we know that because it's biblical.

> *"Be sober and watchful, for your adversary the devil is like a roaring lion and walks about, seeking whom he may devour" (1 Peter 5:8).*

I have two bosses whose lives don't project holiness. They live a life in darkness, which does not please God. One of them in particular uses diabolical tools. The Lord showed me, they use influence and manipulate the people I work with to turn them against me. They have done it so subtly and cunningly that they have wanted to get me out of there, with lies and deceit, especially discriminating for being Hispanic and Christian.

Something that many of us go through in this world, Jesus was discriminated against by his own. Christians are being discriminated against in the military, God showed me, because the enemy is promoting people not to change the course of homosexuality and the laws. He came to his own business, and his own did not receive him.

12 But to all who received him, to those who believed in his name, he gave the right to become children of God; (John 11:11-12 RSV).

But I've been fighting this battle with prayer and fasting. Asking God to convert them and to be a witness to his glory, just as he did with Saul, today known as "Paul." This week, I asked to speak to the greatest commander, the General of my unit. I explained to him what was happening, he is investigating through the department of "Equal opportunity for all," and everything has been high, they do not take me out of any place until everything is resolved.

What I want to convey is that we have rules here on Earth, just as in heaven. I have fasted, prayed, and now I must use the earthly legal departments to continue this earthly fight against discrimination. This place where God has put me makes the enemy uncomfortable.

This territorial place was in need of God's children to intercede for it, to take possession of their territory, and not to be intimidated by anyone, even if they are children of darkness.

The dream was interpreted as follows: I am dealing with people who have satanic influences and who come to curse those who belong to God. That's why they kept telling me, "Bless me! Bless me!" because they are influenced by demons and need to be set free.

The Power of the Tongue

When we speak or wish ill upon our enemy, that immediately becomes a curse. That's why Jesus tells us in His word, in the book of Luke, "Bless those who curse you, pray for those who mistreat you" (Luke 6:28 [KJV]).

That's why in the dream, the person carrying curses wanted to curse me, and when I rebuked them in the name of Jesus, I could see who they were, and they told me to bless them, because enemies are not cursed, they are blessed. Jesus wants to teach us that by blessing, those blessings also become blessings for us.

Jesus blessed all those who wanted to see Him fail. The world is like a magnet; it has attraction. When you say something into the atmosphere, what you say happens. Your words have power. That's why the Bible speaks of the mouth as a fountain of both fresh and bitter water. Read Mark 5:1-9.

Between Two Worlds By Elizabeth Walcott

While I was preaching on the radio, I had the book of Proverbs, but I wanted to share this dream. The Lord instantly told me, "Speak about those who mistreat and revile." Jesus changed my message. When He told me, I opened the Bible and instantly found Luke 6:28-29. When I opened my phone, the same verse appeared. This message is from God.

> *Blessed are you when men hate you, and when they turn you away from themselves, and reproach you, and reject your name as evil, for the sake of the Son of Man. But to you who hear, I say: Love your enemies, do good to those who hate you; 28 Bless those who curse you, and pray for those who slander you. 29 To him that smiteth thee on one cheek, present unto him also the other; and to him who takes away your cloak, do not even deny him your tunic. (Luke 6:22-29)*

The point is that they are cursed and bound and want to be free and blessed, but they can't and don't know how to get our attention to be free. Also remember that I am dealing with people of satanic influence, and that is a reflection that they are doing something against me, but at the same time God showed me that the Power that is in me through the Holy Spirit is greater than that which is in the world, which is not the boss, but the demonic spirit that is using it and man wants to be free.

In the dream I saw how a spirit of cursing took away everyone who was there, except me, because I was blessed with blessings from on high. Now we only have to do two things, one is to forgive and understand that they only do what their father tells them (satan). Second, God shows us what's coming before it comes to us, and he shows us and teaches us what's going on around us before it happens.

If you haven't understood me, I want you to listen to this. When someone rises up against you, it's so that you can help them be free, it's not to make you angry but to bless them and let them be free by the power of the Holy Spirit. You are blessed, it is time to bless your children, spouse, neighbors, your city, nation and everyone who comes into contact with you.

Let us reflect on the power of blessings and curses, which are often spoken aloud to bring about good or evil. In the Hebrew Bible, three key words are frequently used in this context: "alah," "arar," and "killel." The first word, "alah," translates to "curse," and refers to a wish for someone to suffer harm or misfortune. As children of light, we must refrain from wishing harm upon others; otherwise, we risk becoming like the children of darkness. The devil desires to bring evil upon God's children, which is why he attacks them.

Then his wife said to him, *"Do you still retain your integrity?" Curse God, and die,* (Job 2:9).

Curses are pronounced and come from the heart when someone holds a grudge and jealousy towards you. They want the results to be a punishment for you, with the effect of a prohibition or barrier to exclude or anathematize. In other words, satan blames us for his fall, and his destitution from heaven, and because God created us in his image, he is always cursing those of us who are God's children, those whose nation is that of Jacob's God. He is constantly accusing us before God for according to him "our faults" that is why Christ came to shed his blood for us, so that we would have access to the throne of Grace. Since he was there before creation, and saw how God made us, he felt that he too could create a kingdom with his own children and war against the Creator and the one true God. Because the adversary who is satan tempted the woman and she fell, satan believes that he has legacy in God's creation, when Eve sinned.

"Annulling the record of the decrees that was against us, which was contrary to us, he got out of the way and nailed it to the cross" (Colossians 2:14-15).

Our enemy has always wanted to be like God, creating satanic religions, influencing people who worship him, he uses God's creation to build his kingdom. But Apostle Paul in the book of Colossians even in verse 13 (if you read it), you can see that there was a code and regulations that were marking us against God. That is why in verse 15 it says this

"And despoiling principalities and powers, he exhibited them publicly, triumphing over them on the cross."

Christ wrested "ALL" power from the enemy over His creation, and gave it to us to exercise here on earth through Jesus

Christ our Almighty God. We do not belong to the devil or to any principality or nation that is ruled by the devil.

Therefore, the enemy believes himself superior to God, Jesus took away all superiority that ruled over sin in us through the blood of the lamb we are free; Of course we are in this body, of course we live in this world, but we are not subject to it, nor to the flesh, nor to the world. It seems that the enemy got stuck in the Old Testament in Genesis when Adam and Eve sinned. Every legality that the enemy may have over you is broken today!

> *Prayer: Today I declare in the name of Jesus that you are removed, you are never again manipulated by the enemy." Because we are now children of Yahweh, heaven is in our favor. NO more bound to the designs of the flesh or other force of the devil. Every person who makes war on you today is never again used to make war on you, in the name of Jesus.*

Finally, although it has not yet been revealed, we know that to God one day is like a thousand years and one year is like a thousand days. The enemy and his followers have already been forever sent into the abyss into the lake of fire. The future is something that has already been created, God has already affirmed it, if you don't believe me, read the book of Ephesians.

> *9 And to make clear to all what is the dispensation of the mystery hidden from the ages in God, who created all things; 10 that the manifold wisdom of God may now be made*

known through the church to the principalities and powers in the heavenly places, 11 according to the eternal purpose which he made in Christ Jesus our Lord," (Ephesians 3:9-11).

Our Lord Jesus Christ has already declared it, He has already established it, He has already affirmed it. Everything is done and completed according to his will.

We have talked about curses, but God has disturbed me that He speaks to you about blessings. The word blessed in Hebrew (mibtsarah) means strong, fortified tower, fence, castle, or retained wall.

You carry not only the blessings, but you are the blessing, you walk, and as you open your lips, the blessings from on high come out from you to others.

3 Go, behold, I send you out like lambs in the midst of wolves. 4 Do not carry a purse, or a bag, or shoes; and you greet no one on the way. 5 In whatever house you enter, first say, Peace be to this house. 6 And if there be any son of peace there, your peace shall rest upon him; and if not, it will return to you, (Luke 10:3-6).

When someone is in darkness, or trapped in darkness, they are cursed and bear a curse, in the dream I had to describe in this chapter, by rebuking the unclean spirit that this man was being used by satan to curse those of that house and take them away, when he faced me he could not, since the power of the Name that is over every name is within me.

The unclean spirit came out of that man, and the man exclaimed, "Bless me," because he recognized that he needed to be free, but at the same time he wanted the blessings from above. In the book of Luke, our Lord Jesus Christ commanded the disciples two by two, and in verse three, he tells them that he sent them out like sheep in the midst of wolves.

Wolves devastate sheep, they are their worst enemies. I think their favorite food is sheep like we see it in the movies. But that's how Jesus wanted us to identify, that this road is not going to be easy, that we're going to have people waiting for us to pass by to tear off our skin, and everything else, I imagine that the wolf doesn't even leave the blood of the sheep when it eats them.

In verse four of the book of Luke 10:5-7 it tells us that when you enter someone's house and they do not receive you, "listen" this is the most important thing if you feel rejected (a). When they reject you, the blessings that they were going to receive, you will receive, because you bring blessings, you are a door of blessings to the nations.

You carry Jesus and Jesus is blessing and salvation to others, blessings come back to you, so it is very important not to waste your time with someone who you have already shaken your feet; now if God tells you to stay there, it's different, but if he tells you to shake your feet, it's because Jesus has blessed you to follow and bless others, don't waste your time explaining to someone who doesn't want to be blessed. You bring peace and blessings, don't waste them.

The Power of Intercession

Being united in prayer one morning with my intercessory sisters, from the intercessory group, I listened and felt that after praying for a few minutes, we had oppression and war in what we were praying I felt a strange presence next to me and when we joined to pray in tongue I felt how little by little I received strength and something powerful touched me and gave me strength and the strange presence left, That day all of us who are interceding felt that strange presence.

It is important to speak in tongues. Days later, at the end of the Intercessors class to say goodbye, we are interceding and Norita was broken by the Holy Spirit, I immediately felt strong and large wings entering the place where we are interceding, and I said to myself "an angel stood next to me" listen to the Lord who told me, let her unburden herself on me, I felt those wings literally ring, and I felt the powerful presence of God as if He was protecting us and I was listening to Norita and her prayer. I have never seen angels, but it is the first time I have felt an angel stand next to me.

Intersection Tools

One of the most powerful tools is the word of God. This authoritatively declared word comes not only through your lips, but has God's backing. In the book of Isaiah, notice what the Prophet Isaiah says in chapter 55.

10 For as rain and snow come down from heaven, and do not return thither, but water the earth, and cause it to sprout and bring forth, and give seed to the sower, and bread to the eater, 11 so shall my word be that proceedeth out of my mouth; she will not return to me empty, but will do what I will, and will prosper in that for which I sent her, Isaiah 55:10-11.

The prophet who prophesies has to prophesy through the mouth of God, they speak for God, whatever God tells them to speak, they must speak. Prophets are subject to God's obedience and mission here on earth. You have to have complete submission to God; consecrated to God.

What you speak has power, so when we intercede it is very important to know this verse, because there is no one, no matter how much he stands against the will of God, the enemy can try and will try, but it is up to us if we let him do what he wants. God's purpose is going to be fulfilled in a mouth that has power and authority from God, and that knows who He is, so it's very important not to let the flesh take control of your lips, or the emotions take control of your lips. When God's word comes out of your mouth, you're speaking life or death.

Prayer: Father on this day I submit all my organs, including my lips so that they may be your voice here on earth, and that the flesh may not take or ever have control of your will here on earth.

CHAPTER 15
Knowing Your Enemies

As a soldier in the army, I can tell you, the enemy must be known; he cannot be taken for granted, every enemy must know its entrances and exits, its weapons and its allies. In many churches, they don't teach about the enemy, and people are afraid to mention the name of satan, as if he were omnipotent and all-powerful. When there is war, the enemy is studied, to know what his tools are, and his power, as well as to destroy him.

God knows the enemy, and that's why it's so important to know him as well. One of the lies and deceptions that the enemy has been working on many of the church leaders is the fear of mentioning and knowing satan. Satan is not run away, rebuked, and confronted in the name of Jesus, satan is not more powerful than Jesus, if Jesus is within you and his Holy Spirit there is no power that can overcome you, only your worst enemy, "the flesh".

The enemy knows us; that's why he attacks us, and many times, we don't have the tools we need to destroy him. It's because we don't take the time to know his strategies and be able to win those wars that he makes against us. We are fighting from a position of victory won from the future, before the world was made.

We are fighting from an advantageous position, that is why in the spiritual environment it is necessary not to move, because from that position, you and I have already won the battle. No Soldier moves from his position without first consulting with his commanders. Our control tower is God; he is the one who puts us in a certain place because we need to win one or many battles there from a point and place of victory. Wars are won by obedience to the call of the Holy Spirit.

I fear that as the serpent deceived Eve by his cunning, your senses will somehow be led astray from sincere faithfulness to Christ" (2 Corinthians 11:3).

Paul wants to tell us that he fears that people will fall into falsehood and not know God, just as Eve fell into sin and did not know God. The enemy's job is that we do not come to know Christ as He is, nor that we can complete our mission and purpose of God here on earth. Discernment is very important to be able to recognize the enemy's strategies and not be left without knowledge of who Jesus really is.

That is why Jesus said that the Father seeks worshipers who worship him in spirit and in truth, because, by knowing God's deity and his will here on earth, no matter how much the enemy wants to divert you from your purpose and your position of war, he will not be able to because you already know his strategies and by recognizing his strategies you will be able to attack his tools that he uses with against you, without having any effect, because you already recognize them.

The health department injects us with viruses, so that when in the future those viruses want to enter our body, our system recognizes it and at once sends antibodies to attack that virus, your body recognizes it and attacks it at once, sending a signal to where the virus is and how to counteract it.

God has designed us in the same way, that when the enemy attacks you with something that you have already gone through, your spirit and soul are so connected to him that, at once, your senses and spiritual discernment puts you on alert and recognizes where and whom you have to counter, whether it is praying, interceding, meditating on the Word and even fasting to break every chain and be filled with God's presence.

Areas Where the Enemy Attacks You

The military invests heavily in classes designed to help soldiers, and one of these is called **resilience training**. Resilience, in this context, refers to **withstanding adversity**—equipping individuals with the mental, emotional, and psychological tools needed to remain strong amidst discouragement, problems, and other challenges. These classes help soldiers develop a positive and robust mindset, enabling them to combat issues like suicide and family problems.

Practically, it is the ability to get up, to recover after a fall, in which you face pressure, being strong, and getting up "never accepting defeat". The ability to grow in difficult soil. It also teaches five dimensions in which you will have to stay strong: Physical, Emotional, Social, Spiritual, and Family Dimensions. And as I read this, those are the areas that the enemy is constantly attacking; your body with diseases, emotional problems where your mind attacks with thoughts of depression, suicide, and this is created if you make room for those demons. One of the tools to attack your mind is 'accusations', where people stand up to you without you having done much. We see the example in Job and Joshua, the book of Zechariah 3:1-2,

> *Then he showed me Joshua the high priest, who was standing before the angel of the LORD. and Satan was at his right hand to accuse him. And the angel of the LORD said to Satan, "The LORD rebuke you, Satan." Rebuke the LORD who has chosen Jerusalem. Isn't this a brand snatched from the fire?"*

Demons and unclean spirits need bodies in order to function more effectively in our world, they move and get into the available bodies that open the doors to them. That is why a Christian person must have a life filled with the word and glory of God in his life.

Even so, the devil is going to throw out thoughts that hurt our brothers to discourage us and make them shrink from God's purpose, so we must not give room to the enemy and recognize when he is using us as an instrument of his plan. Therefore, every man and woman of

God has to resist the divisions, strife, and misunderstandings of the enemy among the brethren. His plan is to destroy and separate us from God's purpose on earth so that His kingdom may prevail by taking territory from the Kingdom of Christ.

Never let someone take you away or make you angry with someone; try as much as possible to have peace. Now there are many people who are carried away by emotions and do not control their tongue; they have to pray a lot and put themselves in God's hands. Satan is known as the accuser.

And I heard a loud voice in heaven, saying, Now is come, the salvation, and the power, and the kingdom of our God, and the authority of his Christ, for the accuser of our brethren, who accuses them before our God day and night, has been cast down, (Revelation 12:10).

In the emotional areas, he attacks our faith, self-esteem, and problems on a daily basis. if we make the wrong decision, he accuses us and makes us feel the most brutish, inept, without emotional control, defeated, and without faith. If someone sins, whether it is adultery or fornication, we think that this is the most horrible thing that can happen to us, and that God no longer loves us.

That is why many pastors take their own lives. There are many who do not forgive themselves for having an abortion or that the husband has left her for another, or the wife for another. Anxiety is another emotional enemy that is attacking human beings. This is a kind of prison for the one who is in anxiety, many have pills where they never get to recover or cast out that demon.

Social Injustice: We have seen Social Injustice in many places, starting with God's people, where more than six million Jews were unjustly killed, either out of jealousy, hatred, and just for being God's people; We also see Black people who have been unjustly killed by those who simply hated their skin color. How many in God have also been killed, without cause.

There was a law during *"The Age of Lynchings"* where individuals were often killed simply for their race. In some cases, even 10% of white individuals were killed for being in relationships with African Americans. This highlights the ongoing struggle we face, as it reflects the belief that God has chosen us and loves all of His creation. It signifies that the entire human race is loved by God, while the devil despises God's creation. Consequently, the children of darkness oppose the children of light and harbor hatred towards us.

In the book of Nehemiah, chapters one and two, we see Nehemiah praying for God to rebuild the temple and for Jehovah's name to be honored. He asks for success in his endeavors. When the children of light pray for blessings, our heavenly Father, whom we trust, does not withhold them. God desires His people to prosper and for His children to receive rewards, which can disturb the children of darkness.

Between Two Worlds By Elizabeth Walcott

In the book of Luke, Jesus tells a parable after the priests, scribes, and rulers question Him about the authority by which He performs His actions. They ask, "By what authority are You doing these things, and who gave You this authority?" This conversation is recorded in Luke 20. In response, Jesus introduces the story of wicked tenants who mistreat others, which symbolizes His impending persecution here on earth.

Spiritually speaking, being spiritually asleep does not exempt one from attack. On the contrary, every enemy waits quietly, planning how to strike. In sports, there is both a loser and a winner; in this spiritual battle, winning depends on you—not on Jesus. If you seek God, you have the victory; if you do not seek Him, you risk defeat. It is a lie from the very depths of hell to say that God has done everything for us. If that were true, why are we still at war with the devil? We see unsaved children, stagnant church growth, and people working against us.

When you are spiritually asleep, the workers of Satan can infiltrate your life. If you pray, you limit their access to you and your loved ones. However, if you do not pray, God's protective hedge is still there, but how can you truly experience His presence without communion through prayer?

Consider Job: Satan sought permission from God to afflict him because God was protecting him, and Job was a man of prayer. Imagine the enemy surrounding the earth, ready to attack you, while you neglect prayer! Do you think the devil won't say to God, "Let me shake his house, his finances, his health, and his children"? If the enemy was allowed to afflict Job so severely, what might he expect of us? The more we seek God, the greater our assurance that He is with us and protecting us.

If there is no warfare, there is no victory. Enough of the complaints about "the enemy waging war on you." That's what the enemy does; it is his role. Once a cherished and glorious angel, he fell along with a third of the angels due to his pride. When a character has influence, many desire to be like them. However, in the kingdom of God, when a child of God is used by the Holy Spirit, performing miracles and wielding gifts, the enemy will rise up against them—often using sickness, trials, and even the flesh of others.

War is not won through complaints—it is won by battling in the Spirit, using the tools that Jesus left us. The weapons of our warfare are not carnal but are mighty in God for the destruction of strongholds. The enemy targets all of God's creation because he despises the children of light, especially those actively serving in the gifts bestowed upon them by the Holy Spirit.

Changing Your Vocabulary

I don't usually begin my writings by discussing the enemy, but today the Holy Spirit has directed me to address this topic. Often, when we encounter difficulties in our daily lives, we quickly blame the enemy. The words "devil" or "Satan" come to our lips more readily than the names "Jesus" or "God."

Between Two Worlds By Elizabeth Walcott

As warriors of Christ and as children of God, we must remember that our struggle is not against flesh and blood but against principalities and powers of wickedness. However, our greatest enemy is our own flesh. Not everything that happens to us can be attributed to the enemy; it may feel as though everything is going wrong—if it's not one issue, it's another. The Holy Spirit reminds me of the biblical account of King Balak and Balaam, where, despite the enemy's desire to curse God's people, Jehovah chose to bless them. What God has blessed, the enemy cannot curse.

Recently, I have opened doors to preach on the radio in my local area, an FM station. I am also assisting many churches worldwide, which has made the devil uncomfortable. A few days ago, I had a vision of some large, ugly claws that resembled those of a dinosaur with three sharp nails. In the vision, I saw them touching my back.

Soon after, I experienced intense pain in my back that made it difficult to walk or sit for long periods. I visited the doctor and received medication and therapy. Two weeks later, while reading Daniel chapter 10, I was reminded of the struggle Daniel faced during his 21 days of fasting, and how the Archangel Michael had to fight against the prince of Persia in the air. He is the guardian Archangel of the people of Israel. Daniel prayed and fasted to receive the interpretation of a vision.

This illustrates the constant warfare that is a part of every man and woman of God's life. When we let our guard down, the enemy tries to gain a foothold and descend upon us with various tools aimed at the children of light. Yes, I pray and I fast, but I must also recognize that Satan prowls like a roaring lion, seeking someone to devour. He is not playing with us; he hates us and longs to see us destroyed.

God allowed me to experience that vision of the claws to alert me that the enemy was about to attack my body. I did pray that day, but I forgot the vision. It is crucial for us to stay aware of what God reveals to us because it is essential for a warrior to be prepared at all times for what lies ahead.

As every ministry grows, so too will the challenges and wars we face. If you are doing something significant for God and His people, believe me, the enemy will rise up against you. But every man and woman of God must embody the attitude of Paul and Silas; even while in prison, they praised Him!

Even when you are faced with hatred, criticism, and disapproval, keep on praising! The only one who can control your worship and praise of God is you. You have the power to lift your voice in worship, regardless of what you are going through. Just worship, and you will see how our heavenly Father takes delight in your praise.

Victorina Macario has faced many trials while studying at the intercessors' school. She participated in a Zoom meeting led by Barbara Wintrobe, whose ministry focuses heavily on the prophetic. During the meeting, they discussed faith, and it felt as though the message was directed right at her. One of my students was dealing with her brother, who had been unjustly imprisoned.

In that Zoom meeting, God spoke to Macario, indicating that only two of my students could enter. God has ministered to each of my students individually. Sometimes we don't fully understand what God is doing or how He will accomplish it, but if we are determined to let God fulfill His will, everything will ultimately work out as our heavenly Father desires.

The existence of both the spiritual world and the physical world is a fact. Therefore, it is important to remember that whatever we do for others will be returned to us, often in greater measure. As children of God, we are called to project Jesus into the world. Even if we do not receive blessings in return, we must continue to bless others, knowing that we will reap rewards.

Consider Joseph and his eleven brothers: they sold him into slavery, unaware that God was working to fulfill His purpose for him. When someone pushes against you, don't be surprised; it may be God pushing you toward your own purpose. The region benefited from what happened to Joseph. Initially, it seemed that Joseph's dreams would never come true, but that was not the case. God allowed his brothers to sell him so that Joseph could fulfill his destiny.

It is essential for us to endure deception, reproach, and mistreatment as we move toward our purpose and destiny. The enemy may attack us, but God can use those experiences to bless us even more. Look at Job: God permitted him to go through tremendous suffering, but he was ultimately blessed when he forgave and blessed his three friends. You must have the revelation of the law of the harvest; this is why Jesus taught us about sowing and reaping.

When we sow affection and love, we will reap the same in return. However, if we sow gossip and curses, that is what we will harvest. By blessing others, we affirm our identity as children of God and embrace what He has in store for us. Those who criticize you do so out of ignorance; they do not know your past or present. Don't worry about those who push against you, as they may be unknowingly guiding you toward your purpose. This is why it's crucial to love our enemies and bless those who curse us.

In any conflict, there are many strategies for achieving victory. God has His strategies for winning our battles. Jesus utilized prayer and fasting—in preparation from His Father—and relied on the Word to overcome the challenges He faced daily.

David utilized the Mount of Olives, a place associated with oil, as a source of renewal. It requires effort to obtain that spiritual oil. Through prayer and seeking God, David finds strength in the Lord. On the Mount of Olives, he receives revelation. This is also the place where Jesus gathered with the disciples. Both David and Jesus sought refuge in the Father there.

CHAPTER 16
Other Areas of Attack

Apart from the areas of the heart, mind and your physical body; I need you to know that this is not only what the devil attacks with his demons, but that the purpose is to stop your purpose here on earth, to exterminate you completely, and to plunder the spoils. If we could elaborate like this, a thief comes to steal and destroy your purpose so you cannot lose this battle, the battle is not only here on earth but in the atmosphere. If you lose your battleground, you will lose your battleground with Christ when He comes to fight and utterly destroy Satan's kingdom.

As a soldier and a child of God, I encourage you to immerse yourself in the waters of the Holy Spirit. Another attack that the enemy uses that is not mentioned much is social media. On social media he puts your name on lists of elite agents apart from the Antichrist's agenda, if you put anything that is related to God, you immediately become an enemy of social media, not of those who support you but of those who have created those social networks. A great persecution approaches those who have social networks that manifest in great power of the Holy Spirit, those who genuinely want to see the unsaved people know God.

When Jesus began his ministry, the first one instituted his apostles, but he also had his disciples, John also had disciples. The circle of influence is very common among fraternities in the United States. The Freemasons, Esther Stars and the fraternity between Brothers (Alpha, Beta, Chi) even within the armed forces; We also see this in government, where businesses, positions, jobs depend on who you know. Don't underestimate the power of influence.

When someone knows you, your name is resonant or between these circles you are worth nothing or you are worth a lot. I have seen and experienced that when I recommend someone, God does something particular in that person, gives him his favor, gives him the job, promotes him. Because the power of the circle of influence that Jehovah's sons have is very similar to that of men here on earth. I am writing this book and I feel a unique and unparalleled power in the center of my stomach, because there are many who are losing this battle, because they have not learned to relate to the Holy Spirit so that He will be the one to relate you to people who are also full of Him.

Jesus was teaching many, but in certain places he could not do miracles as he wanted because of his influence in that region, he was despised, so he said that he had not been able to do miracles in that region because of lack of unbelief and belief; for only being the son of Joseph, the carpenter?

22 They all bore good witness to him and were amazed at the gracious words that came out of his mouth. They said, "Isn't this Joseph's son?" 23 He said to them, "Surely you will tell me this saying: 'Physician, heal yourself. Of so many things that we have heard that have been done in Capernaum, do also here in your land." 24 And he added, "Truly I say to you, no prophet is welcome in his own land" (Luke 20:22-24).

I hear the Holy Spirit tell me that he writes about legality. "Legality" there are certain spirits that have authorized themselves in legality over certain regions, since the church has not taken away his regime in that region, the devil knows when a child of God enters those regions, institutions, that he has declared to be his.

Their demons assigned in certain places know each other and feel uncomfortable when someone comes anointed by the power of the Holy Spirit, their diabolical influence works orderly to stop the movement of God and the will of God on earth and those particular regions. In that circle of influence he uses human bodies since he cannot do anything without a human body; Unfortunately the church has been losing territory by being distracted in four walls with programs that have no influence on the spiritual world.

Wasting time are many arguing and fighting among themselves, "who is better, who has the biggest, most powerful, full church;" And they have forgotten that the vision and mission of the church is not within four walls, but in instituting his Kingdom and destroying Satan's kingdom here on earth. His kingdom here on the earth of Jesus Christ was already won on the cross, but the job of us as His ambassadors is to continue to advance the Kingdom of Light that is Jehovah, in counteracting the kingdom of darkness that is Satan.

Many institutions and fraternities use books to have influence over people, institutions, but at the same time they use the circle of influence between them, they use their ranks, they use the internet/platform to collaborate with each other, they use their friendships and friends to get jobs and positions. And the church? Fighting with each other, jealousy with each other, striving with each other and criticizing when God lifts someone up and uses them for His glory.

We have to learn a lot, we have lost a lot of territory, because we are letting demonic spirits influence us and destroy someone with their tongue. On this day I want to give you some advice, leave strife and strife with one another, and join one who is doing the will of God, preach the gospel, prophesy, teach the word to many, and let us stop being used by the enemy; submit the flesh to the will of God and let us leave the ministerial strife and jealousy.

Jesus' circle was the most powerful and needy in that age than ever before. Every man and woman of God should have a circle of brothers where he or she can call and know that when two or three join in his or her name, there will be My Father; not to destroy another brother or sister but so that the works of hell will recede from your home, your work, your region and country.

Many angry with each other, it is not worth fighting with someone who is in the Kingdom of God, shake that, it is enough that satan seeks us to kill us. Don't be a Soldier who kills his own fellow militiamen. Be someone who uses the power of prayer, word, and blood to thwart the devil, his demons, and minions. If the unsaved know how to help his friends, how much more so do we who are supposed to be of the Kingdom of heaven and the earth of Jehovah.

Prayer: Father, I ask you to help me remove from my mind and heart the singular mentality, and enter the plural and Kingdom mentality; that I do not allow myself to be influenced by the gossip of others who have spoken ill of someone and that I know what your perfect will is in my city, and the whole region of this country. I uproot all satanic influences that do not allow me to see with the spiritual eyes of the kingdom. From this day on I declare that I never again have a singular church mentality, but that I have a Kingdom mentality and do things in the circle of Jehovah and his children. May my influence be your power that comes from the Holy Spirit and from my brothers who help each other every day on a global and regional level.

The most influential and powerful name that ever existed is Jesus, Yeshua. There is no other name in the heavens, or on earth, or under like the name of our savior. The people of Israel rejected Jesus, they do not know what they missed, Jesus met with them, they were able to see him face to face in person, hear his voice, see all the wonderful miracles in person and in full color, without binoculars Jesus himself walked among them and they did not recognize him.

I know that you would like, even if it is for a few minutes, to be able to live that moment, its miracles, imagine when the woman with the issue of blood touches Jesus and immediately she receives power and healing. When the loaves and fishes Jesus cuts off a piece and suddenly the bread grows again, or when he cuts the fish and the tail comes out again, or when he calls Lazarus and Lazarus comes out of the tomb tied in those gauzes and cloaks, and see Mary and Martha look on their faces when their brother is resurrected.

Also to see Mary as a mother, to see her son as he accepted the will of the Father, to die for us on the cross, where the cross was one of the most tortuous deaths that ever existed. Knowing that you were the one who would have to be there, what would you tell Mary? That is why I say to you do not take the blood of Jesus in vain, let him who sins sin less.

David's Army

Please read in 1 Chronicles 12, the Lord trained David's men here on earth to win wars in the physical world. In the same way in the spiritual world we have Angels that must be activated in our favor. Read also Hebrews 12:5-8, Numbers 22:22-35, 1 Timothy 2:4.

David, proclaimed king of Israel, 1 Chronicles 1:1-31

1 Then all Israel gathered around David in Hebron and said to him, "We are your bone and your flesh. 2 Even before now, while Saul reigned, you were the one who brought Israel out to war and brought them back. Also the Lord your God has said to you: "You shall feed my people Israel, and you shall be prince over Israel, my people. 3 And all the elders of Israel came before the king at Hebron. David made a covenant with them before the Lord, and they anointed David king over Israel through Samuel, according to the word of the Lord. David takes the fortress of Zion. 4 Then David went with all Israel to Jerusalem, which is Jesus. and the Jebusites dwelt in that land. 5 And the inhabitants of Jesus said to David, "You shall not enter here." But David took the stronghold of Zion, which is the City of David. 6 David had said, "Whoever first defeats the Jebusites will be the head and the leader." Then Joab son of Zeruiah went up first, and was made chief. 7 David took up residence in the fortress, and for this reason they called it the City of David. 8 He built the city around it, from Milus to the wall; and Joab repaired the rest of the city. 9 And David went on and on, and the LORD of hosts was with him.

`David's Brave

10 These are the leaders of the mighty men that David had, who helped him in his kingdom, together with all Israel, to make him reign over Israel, according to the word of the Lord. 11 This is the list of David's mighty men: Jasobeam son of Hacmoni, leader of the thirty, who once brandished his spear against three hundred, and killed them. 12 After him was Eleazar son of Dodo the Ahhite, who was of the three mighty men. 13 He was with David at Pasdamim, where the Philistines had gathered for battle. There was a plot of land full of barley, and when the people fled before the Philistines, 14 he stood in the middle of the plot, defended it, and defeated the Philistines, for the Lord favored them with a great victory. 15 Three of the thirty leaders went down to the rock to meet David, to the cave of Adullam, when the Philistines' camp was in the valley of Rephaim. 16 David was in the fortress at the time, while a garrison of the Philistines was occupying Bethlehem. 17 David said, "Would that I could drink from the waters of the well of Bethlehem, which is at the gate!" 18 And these three broke into the camp of the Philistines, drew water from the well of Bethlehem, which is at the gate, and took it and brought it to David. but he would not drink it, but poured it out for the Lord, and said, 19 "May my God keep me from doing this. Am I going to drink the blood and life of these men who have brought it at the risk of their lives?" And he didn't want to drink it. This is what those three brave men did. 20 Ahiab's brother Abishai was the leader of the thirty. Once, he swung his spear at three hundred men and killed them. Thus he gained renown among the three. 21 He was the most illustrious of the thirty, for he became their leader, but he did not equal the first three. 22 Benaiah son of Jehoiada was the son of a mighty man from Kabzeel, who was of great deeds. he overcame the two lions of Moab; He also descended and killed a lion in a pit, in the middle of a snowfall. 23 He himself defeated an Egyptian, a man five cubits in height; And the Egyptian had a spear like a weaver's roller, but he came down with a stick, and snatched the spear from the Egyptian's hand and killed him with his own spear. 24 Benaiah son of Jehoiada did this and made a name for himself among the three mighty men. 25 He was the most distinguished of the thirty, but he did not equal the first three. He put David in his personal guard. 26 The mighty men of the hosts were: Asahel the brother of Joab, Elhanan the son of Dodo, the one of Bethlehem, 27 Shamoth the Harodite, Helesh the Pelonite; 28 Ira the son of Ichesh, the Tekoite, Abiezer, the Anatotite, 29 Sibecai the Husthite, Ilai the Ahhite, 30 Mahahai the Netophathite, Heled the son of Baanah, the Netophatite, 31 Ittai the son of Ribai, of Gibeah, of the Benjamin, Benaiah, the Pirathonite, 32 Hurai of the river Gaash, Abiel the Arbatite, 33 Azmaveth, the Barhumite, Eliaba the Saalbonite, 34 the sons of Hasem, the Gizonite, Jonathan the son of Sage the Ararite, 35 Ahiam the son of Schar the Ararite, Eliphah the son of your, 36 Hepher the Mecheratite, Ahijah the Pelonite, 37 Hezro the Carmelite, Naarai the son of Ezbai, 38 Joel the brother of Nathan, Mibhar the son of Hagrai, 39 Shelk the Ammonite, Naharai the Beerothite, armor-bearer of Joab the son of Zeruiah, 40 Ira the Ythite, Gareb the Ythite, 41 Uriah the Hittite, Zabad the son of Ahlai, 42 Adina the son of Siza the Reubenite, the prince of the Reubenites, and thirty men with him, 43 Hanan the son of Maacah, Jehoshaphat the Mithite, 44 Uzziah the Ashtarotite, and Shamah and Jehiel the sons of Hotham the Aroerite; 45 Jedia the son of Shimri, and Joha his brother the Zhikite, 46 Eliel the Mahavite, Jerebai and Jehosavaya the sons of Elnaam, Itma the Moabite, 47 Eliel, Obed, and Jaasiel the Mesobaite.

Then in 2 Chronicles 23:1-21 it continues saying,

In the seventh year, Jehoiada took courage, and took hundreds of captains: Azariah son of Jeroham, Ishmael son of Johanan, Azariah son of Obed, Maaseiah son of Adaiah, and Elishaphat son of Zichri, who made a covenant with him. And they went through Judah and gathered together the Levites from all the cities of Judah and the heads of the fathers' houses of Israel, and they came to Jerusalem. Then the whole assembly made a covenant with the king in the house of God. And Jehoiada said to them, "Behold, the king's son will reign, just as the LORD has spoken concerning the sons of David." This is what you shall do: A third of you, of the priests and Levites who enter the Sabbath day, shall be gatekeepers; another third part will be in the king's house, and another third part in the Puerta del Cimiento; and all the people shall be in the courts of the house of the LORD. But let no one enter the house of the LORD except the priests and Levites who minister; These can enter because they are holy. And let all the people keep the precept of the LORD. The Levites will surround the king, each with his weapons in his hand; and anyone who enters the house will be killed. You will be with the king when he enters and when he comes out. And the Levites and all Judah did according to all that Jehoiada the priest had commanded. Each of them took his men, those who were to enter on the Sabbath, together with those who were to leave on the Sabbath, because Jehoiada the priest did not send any of the groups away. Then Jehoiada the priest gave to the captains of hundreds the spears and shields, large and small, which had belonged to King David, which were in the house of God. And he placed all the people, every man with his weapon in his hand, from the right side of the house to the left side of the house, by the altar and by the house, around the king. Then they brought out the king's son and put the crown on him, gave him the book of testimony, and made him king. And Jehoiada and his sons anointed him, and cried out, Long live the king! When Athaliah heard the noise of the people running and praising the king, she went to the people in the house of the LORD, and looked, and behold, the king was standing by his pillar at the entrance, and the captains and the trumpets were standing by the king. And all the people of the land rejoiced and blew trumpets, and the singers with their musical instruments led the praise. Then Athaliah tore her clothes, and cried, "Treachery!" Treason! But Jehoiada the priest brought out the captains of hundreds who were in command of the army, and said to them, "Bring her out from among the ranks; and whoever follows her, kill him with the sword. For the priest had said, "Do not kill her in the house of the LORD." And they laid hands on her, and when she came to the entrance of the

Horse Gate of the king's house, there they killed her. Then Jehoiada made a covenant between all the people and the king that they would be the people of the LORD. And all the people went to the house of Baal and tore it down, smashed its altars and its images to pieces, and killed Mattan the priest of Baal before the altars.

And Jehoiada placed the offices of the house of the LORD under the authority of the Levitical priests, whom David had appointed over the house of the LORD to offer the burnt offerings of the LORD, as it is written in the law of Moses, with gladness and with songs according to David's command. He set up gatekeepers at the gates of the house of the LORD, so that no one would enter who was unclean for any reason. He took the captains of hundreds, the nobles, the rulers of the people, and all the people of the land, and brought down the king from the house of the LORD, and they entered through the upper gate into the king's house. And they seated the king on the royal throne. And all the people of the land rejoiced, and the city was quiet, because Athaliah had been slain by the sword. (2 Chronicles 23:1-21)

CHAPTER 17
Men Prepared For Spiritual Warfare

The Lord has me in the book of 1 Chronicles 11:12, where it is necessary to emphasize the life of Jehoiada, whom the Bible puts as a brave man. By opening my Dictionary, it was opened exactly in the life of this man. (1 Chronicles 11; 12 [RVR]); 2 Chronicles 23:1-21. I know you've heard, maybe from the 300 movie, about some warriors. They are strong and brave men who fought intensively. But this time I want to talk to you about David's men.

David had many men who fought hard; he had in particular, Benaiah son of Jehoiada, According to the dictionary, Jehoiada was a brave man. David was a warrior, a sheep herder, son, husband, and king. But in all those charges, he was a man who loved God, to the point of calling him "after the heart of God." David sinned, fled, and hid so that Saul would not kill him since Saul was jealous of him. He had many victories, but many of those victories were because he had many people around him and in his charge, many were warriors who were with him in battles. In the book of Chronicles 12:17 NLT, I am impressed that God in verse 17 says:

> *17 When David saw them, he went out to meet them and said, "If your intentions are good and you come to help me, I accept with all my heart that you join my troops; but if they want to betray me and hand me over to my enemies, may our God punish them! I have harmed no one, because I am not a criminal.*

Not everyone can be in your circle of influence or friends. David made it clear to them that if they had evil intentions that God was going to punish them.

In this film (300) the father teaches him never to give up, never to back down against his enemies, he was trained against all kinds of times, during the cold he learned to survive, in times of hunger, killing animals in the forest in order to eat and survive. He learned not to be afraid of anything or anyone.

This is the physical world, but if we transform it into the spiritual world; our Heavenly Father has equipped us with all the necessary tools to be able to resist, not win, because Jesus Christ has already won the war, it is up to us to resist the Devil and his followers and he will flee from us. When a believer says that Jesus has already won the battle, I would like to ask them, in what area did Jesus win the battle?

Because you and I are here still fighting against the enemies of our soul. If you haven't noticed, this phrase "Jesus has already won the battle" is used by many, but they don't understand the meaning. Let me put it in the real perspective. The battle you are fighting is for your life and yours, your ministry, your neighborhood, and the souls that have to come to Christ. In case you didn't know...

> *29 For those whom he foreknew, he also predestined to be conformed to the image of his Son, that he might be the firstborn among many brethren. 30 And those whom he predestined, these he also called; and those whom he called, these he also justified; and those whom he justified, these he also glorified, (Romans 8:28-30, KJV).*

What is the image of Christ? It is not only to be a pastor, to operate in the five calls and gifts of the Holy Spirit to us, but to operate from your place or office, whether it is pastoral, educational, prophetic, evangelical, and apostolic. Your image must be and project Jesus; many stay in the picture of compassion, but isn't that all Jesus did here on earth?

He delivered and healed many of ailments, taught and discipled many, but the main thing is that he did the Father's will. What is the Father's will for your life? What area should you be working on? Not in the church, because we're very good at working in the church, but in the kingdom of Jesus Christ. In the previous chapters I spoke of the "singular" mentality. It's a mind that thinks only of him or her or your local church. You're not here to serve in the church only, you're here because you're the church, the four walls isn't the church, the church is "YOU." If you've heard many say... ! The church is cold, in other words, that the church is not taking possession of God's vision here on earth. That expression is for you, it's "YOU" when you speak and hear about the church not doing anything here on earth, That's You!

Many are afraid of the enemy, but they are very busy, watching television for hours, so you will not have the mentality of the Kingdom, nor will you equip yourself with the power of God. Watching videos and the internet for hours, and criticizing others is not going to lead you to the image of Jesus Christ either. Jesus withdrew to pray in intimacy with the Father, not ten minutes, not five, nor when he saw miracles did he stop praying, but he was constant, he is and was the word here on earth who walked among us and became flesh to do the will of the Father.

What is the Father's will for "You" and don't tell me what the gifts are, because it's not, the gifts are irrevocable, that is, many have gifts and operate in those gifts, but many will not enter the kingdom of heaven; because gifts are a gift from God. There are many who operate in the gifts, and live a sinful life, with pornography, lust, envy, and God uses them with power, because "the gifts are irrevocable (Romans 11:29 KJV). God is pleased to use them, but what is God's will over your life? It is not being a pastor or an evangelist or operating in ministries. What is God's will for your life?

Between Two Worlds By Elizabeth Walcott

It's Simple but Very Delicate

"The Kingdom of Jehovah established here on earth as it is in heaven." (Matt. 6:10) That's God's will for everyone here on earth, because the first Adam gave him to the devil, but the second Adam got him back, that is "Jesus Christ."

From the time John the Baptist began preaching until now, the kingdom of God advances in spite of its enemies. Only brave and determined people manage to be part of it.

13 God had already foretold in the Bible everything that was going to happen, up to the time John the Baptist came, Matthew 11:11-13 (NLT).

That's simple, Jesus snatched the keys from the Devil, and he also conquered death. I mean, you and I have to move forward against the enemies and only those who have decided to fight and be brave. In other words, those who kill bone flesh, your flesh, laziness, your singular or local mind-form, are the ones who can overcome.

People who allow themselves to be dominated by the opinions of others will not be able to advance against the kingdom of satan, people who have been influenced by gossip and slander towards others, and continue to criticize others, i.e. the carnal emotions of the mind and reach the heart, I am not only talking about adultery or fornication or the outward appearance of man, but you allow yourself to be manipulated by others.

The Holy Spirit is speaking to someone to let go of what you think you know and take the "KINGDOM" mentality that is, the mentality of Christ in doing the will of the Father here on earth is what Jesus did, not to operate only in the gift, but to fulfill the will of the Father; to snatch the kingdom of Satan "which the Lord permitted him" that Adam gave in the garden of Eden to the devil.

8 He who practices sin is of the devil; because the devil sins from the beginning. For this purpose the Son of God appeared, to destroy the works of the devil" (1 John 3:8).

Jesus Christ came to undo the works of the devil, you and I are here to continue to reinforce that here on earth, that is your calling, your duty. You've already been equipped, to follow that command of Jesus Christ here on earth. Jesus has already undone that command here but unfortunately the kingdom of darkness is moving forward because he was cast out here on earth, and he is making and establishing his kingdom and having man in darkness, because not everyone is saved, but salvation is for everyone, those who have to be added to the Kingdom of Light that is Christ Jesus.

It is a constant fight where the mighty have to snatch, uproot, establish, decree, rebuke, and take absolute control of the kingdom of darkness through the blood of the Lamb, the word and the name that is above every name; though it has not yet been manifested nor have we seen Jesus in full, your calling and duty is greater than what you have already seen, establishing the Kingdom of Jesus Christ here on earth.

However, as long as one has a "singular or local" mentality, he will never be able to attain the fullness of the totalitarian Kingdom against the hosts of evil operating in your atmospheric region. God is so big that he doesn't fit in the world, but so big that he fits in our hearts, that means that we are not just anything. That is why God does not dwell in temples made with hands, but that temple is made by him and he lives in us. The temple in which he dwells was made by himself, so that he himself might live in it. In us there is eternity, he created us, that is why the enemy fights against the eternal, because he hates everything that is life. What we have to give you, if even we are yours?

A Weapon of War

Satan's weapons are powerful when you allow yourself to be dominated by them, when he turns his demons against you, and you allow yourself to be won and influenced. When God gives you your assignment He will oppose what God is going to do through you. The enemy that if he stops you and makes you waver in God's purposes, he has already won.

When soldiers go to attack the enemy, they expect to attack at the enemy's weakest moments. Every earthly or spiritual realm studies its enemies in order to attack at the most vulnerable moment, to attack its enemies. Studying and knowing your enemy is a very powerful weapon, that is why many preachers today and before have triumphed because they knew their enemies and attacked them in the weakest moments.

The armed forces of many countries when they go to war the purpose is to kill the strongest, the generals, the infantry and the president himself, who is the primary objective, so when there is war the first one they take out to escape is the president. You have to study your enemies, both physical and spiritual, very deeply; physicists because many times we blame the enemy when it is simply someone who is envious of you, and the devil is not even there and has not sent any demons.

The physical enemies with the flesh, many times your own flesh does not want to pray, does not want to fast, does not want to subdue the tongue, and even because it is a very small member you have not held it, many like or love the "gossip", but they blame the devil on those who hang out with them.

Other powerful tools of the enemy are laziness, discouragement, lack of faith, envy and ministerial zeal, depression, apathy to the things of God. The enemy is going to send his demons at every moment, but I have seen more of their attacks when the body is resting because there are movements in the heavens and they (the demons) stand in the way of the work of God and the advance of the Kingdom of Jesus Christ seems more during the early morning, when everything is quiet, waiting for us to sleep, that is why the Lord raises his intercessors to pray at 3 am because it is a spiritual tool to intercede at dawn. It's like rush hour. The enemy has tried to close the doors, preventing me from returning to the things of God, and the devil does not want me to walk in God's purpose. When the enemy wants me to back down, it's because God is about to grant us victory.

In the battles I've faced with people who allow themselves to be used by Satan, it may seem as though I have lost the war. However, the lesson is that I am being trained for a greater work of God. The bigger battles are given to the soldiers who are stronger in Christ. The more intense the attack feels, the more God is preparing you to advance further, and soon, victory will be evident.

Never think that just because something God wanted to do in you did not go as you expected, it means that the devil has won. Instead, it is God teaching you and making you stronger and more agile, so that you can win future battles. Many billionaires had to try their products over and over again before achieving great results.

Take Michael Jordan, the most famous basketball player in the United States, as an example. Initially, he did not pass his basketball tryouts or win many medals. He faced rejection because of his height; he was considered too small, and his best friend was chosen over him for the team, putting him in the minor leagues. That was a defeat for Michael, but he viewed it as a challenge. Every time someone rejected him, he saw it as an opportunity to prove himself. Today, Michael Jordan's net worth is more than 3.5 billion dollars.

CHAPTER 18

You Are A Weapon Of War
Against The Kingdom Of Darkness

You are before weapons were invented, you were already formed before your mother had you, before they said she is a girl or a boy, Jehovah had already appointed you to be first his son, and then an instrument in his hands to undo the works of the enemy.

> *20 You are a hammer to me, and weapons of war; and through you I will break nations, and through you I will destroy kingdoms, (Jeremiah 51:20 KJV).*

What kind of weapons am I referring to? The book of Jeremiah is a prophetic book written by a prophet named Jeremiah, in this chapter 51 we see how Jehovah tells Jeremiah that he is going to raise a wind:

> *15 He is the one who made the earth by his power, who established the world with his wisdom, and stretched out the*

heavens with his understanding. 16 At his voice there are tumults of water in the heavens, and he brings up the clouds of the ends of the earth; he makes lightning out of the rain, and draws the wind out of his storehouses, (Jeremiah 51:15-16).

You are here so that the works of darkness do not prevail, so that the kingdom of darkness does not continue its expansion here on earth, to bring justice from God, since we are his children and everything that darkness does we bring before God in judgment, that is why a Christian cannot mix with the things of this world, because it becomes a Babylon, it is an enemy of light.

Now, what are your weapons? Let's start with your mouth, your mouth is such a powerful instrument that what you declare, proclaim, and say in the spiritual atmosphere through the authority of Christ happens here on earth. In fact, you cause heaven and earth to come together and do the Father's will here on earth. Your voice is a trumpet that sounds in the atmosphere, and you align God's here on earth, that is why the powers of the hosts of wickedness want to take you out of your region, from your work, and from your house, they want to strip you of what has already been predestined before the foundation of the world for you and your ministry.

Never let the enemy shut your mouth, nor let him stop God's purpose that you have to do here on earth. An apparent defeat does not mean that you are going to live from defeat to defeat, as it can be that a man like Michael Jordan, who does not know God has a winning attitude despite trials and defeats, today he is the most powerful and recognized man in history.

How is it that the children of darkness are stronger and braver than many who are trying to enter the kingdom of heaven. Our heavenly Father has not created losers, because he cannot create something that he is not, Jehovah our father has never lost any battle, if you learn to see every obstacle as a goal to be won, you will be able to face the lies and snares of the enemy here on earth, and you will be able to stand firm to counter spiritual warfare.

Massive Military Operations

The army's combined forces conduct unified ground operations to establish operating environments, prevent conflicts, consolidate achievements, and contribute to victory in national wars. Command and control, the exercise of authority and direction by an appropriately appointed commander, is important for all operations during these periods of armed conflict or proxy struggle. "Mission" command is the Army's approach to exercising command and control, based on the vision of war and the nature of operations. The mission command approach emphasizes decentralized execution that is appropriate to the situation and strengthens subordinate decision-making.

The framework used by the military to organize itself and implement control and command are operations. The main command and control activities performed during operations are planning, preparation, execution and continuous evaluation. With the support of their staff, commanders use the operations process to understand, visualize, and describe their operating environments; making and articulating decisions; direct, lead, and evaluate military operations. The Army shapes global security and the global environment while continuously preparing for large-scale ground combat. All military operations follow this process. They describe a mission-type command approach to planning, preparing, executing, and evaluating.

As we can see the operations are well organized, they have someone who directs, in our case it would be the Holy Spirit, the preparation is extensive, it cannot stop the vision and mission of the commander, but the life of many people depends on you pastor, leader, teacher, evangelist. This operates in a global environment, combats that affect the atmosphere, if we are not prepared, we will lose the war. How so? If you don't do what the Father has commanded you to do here on earth, your squadron is going to die, the souls are going to die, they're not going to come to Christ because they're bound.

1. Planning: is the art of science understanding the situation and envisioning the future desire and effectively laying the foundation and structure.

> *49 But he who heard and did not do is like a man who built his house on the ground without foundation; against which the river beat with a rush, and immediately fell, and great was the ruin of that house" (Luke 6:49).*

Jesus is our foundation and sure base, Jesus is the word itself incarnate, The Father has already laid the foundation on this earth, as well as in the spiritual; all are subject to the name which is above every name "Jesus Christ." To man sinning, Jesus was and is the second Adam as it says in Scripture. Let's not be ignorant of our adversary who plans every day how to attack us and destroy God's purpose for our lives. He plans our downfall, our discouragement by bringing unclean spirits when we are asleep, either physically or spiritually.

2. Prepare: These are those activities carried out by units and soldiers to improve their ability to execute an operation. Prepare to evaluate yourself, know what your weakness is and strengthen that weakness, for example, if your weakness is the lack of prayer and not getting up in the early hours of the morning to pray, then you must prepare your mind and your body to get up to pray, you must create a routine or desire to get up early and go to bed early so that your body adapts and has strength to pray at dawn mentally you need to be rigid, agile and motivated to pray, what motivates you here in the world? To see the free souls? Then get ready.

Let them be your children, your husband, so use that to motivate you not to falter in constant prayer; If praying and always stopping praying is fickle, then you will be fickle in everything else, your college homework, or you will never undertake anything in life because you don't want responsibility. Jesus was trained from a child in the law, Paul was instructed from his childhood. An athlete prepares to win and have a medal, he does not prepare to lose, a Christian must prepare for the calling and be used here on earth, not for the coming of God, but for God's plan and design here on earth to continue to advance.

Remember that Jesus was made man for the atonement of our sins, he was killed because it was the divine plan of the Father for us to be redeemed through his blood, his death and resurrection; that was the Father's plan for Jesus. A soldier prepares to fight his enemies at any moment, the soldier prepares for war, not for himself, but for the dynamic operations that come where he needs the commander so that at any time he is called, the "YA" is ready.

Although the phrase "Christ is coming soon" may be based on Scripture, many people use it as a cheap excuse to do nothing in the kingdom of God. This causes people not to prepare themselves to conquer souls, nor to live a life of victory in the Kingdom of God. For many years the church keeps saying "Christ is coming!" "Christ Is Coming!" That has caused a unique cooling and laziness not to seek God effectively; that Christ is coming, he is coming!, but what have you done with the gifts and calling that Jehovah has sent you here on earth? Where are the souls you have won? Where are your garments and your crown, which are the works done here on earth?

The devil and his followers prepare daily how to destroy you, and you, what are you preparing for? Are you in theological school? Are you in seminaries? Are you reading books to receive more of His wisdom? Where's your preparation? Is your calling as an evangelist or missionary already getting underway? Are you ready to pray and fast for your own and the nations? How long will you continue in that mentality of only being led by a pastor? your calling is very important, age has no limit, as long as you have air in your lungs, God can still use you.

A soldier gets up and even if it's 10 minutes of prayer each day added to his prayers in the room alone with God. The kingdom of God suffers violence and only the violent snatch it away, rise up and walk in the power of their strength, rise up and leave the excuses, and preach the gospel to all nations, beginning with your nation.

Without preparation there is no victory, without a strong mind to achieve what God has commanded you, you will not be able to, because many want God to do everything, "The Holy Spirit is your helper" Do not have the Holy Spirit as a lucky charm, "is it that God helps me" And you? What do you do to decide to fill yourself with Him, in the early mornings, He is waiting for you, for you to get up, what are you waiting for, when you are 100 years old? Do today what God commanded you to do here on earth and in the Kingdom of Christ before the foundation of the world.

Joseph was prepared by God in prison, when God's plan in his life was the dream he had, his brothers laughed including his father Jacob and his brothers hated him and were carried away by jealousy and envy. Sleep + envy + prison = promotion and God's plan fulfilled.

Don't tell everyone about the dreams you have, pray first, ask the Holy Spirit who is showing you and then you can say it. Remember that unclean spirits cannot be in the holy of holies, because they were removed from what was their place with God before.

> *5 Salmon was Boaz's father, and his mother was Rahab. Boaz was the father of Obed; the mother was Ruth. Obed was the father of Jesse, 6 and Jesse was the father of King David, (Matthew 1:5).*

Rahab was according to here on earth a harlot, but according to God's true purpose she was numbered in the lineage of Jesus. She saw the opportunity and took that opportunity so that her lineage would have a new opportunity and future. God saw a David inside her, even though the man saw a dirty woman.

Esther was prepared for marriage to the king of Ahasuerus: "It came to pass in the days of Ahasuerus, Ahasuerus, who reigned from India to Ethiopia over a hundred and twenty-seven provinces" (Esther 1:1). Esther was queen of twenty-seven provinces. Do you think that if my husband tells me that he is king of twenty-seven provinces, they will come here?, do you think that I would say "No!" Vashti was crazy, with a man of that caliber, I wash him up to his feet! So Esther would impersonate someone she would never imagine; despite being an orphan, God prepared her by using Mordecai as an example for God's work so that one day she would take that position as queen in a palace. God had a plan with her.

It is necessary to understand that the people you have next to you, whether they are church members or family members, you have to educate them to discover, grow and fulfill God's purpose for their lives. A mature Pastor does not treat the members as sheep, but treats them as children of the Kingdom of Jesus Christ, you have to change that mentality and as the Word says, let the five ministries of Jesus Christ be exercised in the church.

David was prepared in the field, in the forest, he had practicing how to kill and defend his sheep, he was a shepherd of sheep, but also a king, a teacher, a warrior, a prophet, a father and a friend. When his enemies like Saul wanted to kill him, he knew how to find refuge in the home of the prophet Samuel.

> *19 And word was given to Saul, saying, Behold, David is at Naioth in Ramah. 20 Then Saul sent messengers to bring David, and they saw a company of prophets prophesying, and Samuel standing there and presiding over them. And the Spirit of God came upon Saul's messengers, and they also prophesied. 21 When Saul heard about it, he sent other messengers, who also prophesied. And Saul sent messengers a third time, and they also prophesied. 22 Then he himself went to Ramah; And when he came to the great well that is in Sheku, he asked, "Where are Samuel and David?" And one answered, "Behold, they are in Naioth in Ramah." 23 And he went to Naioth in Ramah; and the Spirit of God also came upon him, and he kept walking and prophesying until he came to Naioth in Ramah. 24 And he also stripped off his garments, and prophesied likewise before Samuel, and was naked all that day*

and all that night. Hence it was said, "Is Saul also among the prophets?" (1 Samuel 19:19-24).

David knew that the last place Saul would look for him would be among the prophetic like the place of Ramah, where the prophet Samuel and the prophets resided, but if Saul still came, the hand of Jehovah would protect him. When someone is looking for you to kill you either physically or in the spirit, because we do not fight against blood or flesh, but we must understand that everything that moves in the spiritual world is subject to the authority of the name that is above every name, "Jesus". Whether they be principalities, hosts of wickedness, powers, or satanic kingdoms, they have been deprived of all authority that they had, for those who walk in the power and authority of the Kingdom of God are His children, "who are washed with the blood, and their name is written in the book of life." We have power and authority over those demons. Now you should also know that the agreement is very important.

12 For we wrestle not against flesh and blood, but against principalities, against powers, against the rulers of the darkness of this world, against spiritual wickedness in the heavenly places. 13 Therefore take up the whole armor of God, that you may be able to endure in the evil day, and when all is finished, you may stand. 14 Stand therefore, girded with the truth, and put on the breastplate of righteousness, 15 and with the preparation of the gospel of peace. 16 Above all, take up the shield of faith, so that you may quench all the fiery darts of the evil one. 17 And take up the helmet of salvation, and the sword of the Spirit, which is the word of God; 18 praying at all times with all prayer and supplication in the Spirit, and watching over it with all perseverance and supplication for all the saints" (Ephesians 6:12-18).

19 Again I say to you, if two of you agree on earth about anything they ask, it will be done for them by my Father who is in heaven. 20 For where two or three are gathered together in my name, there am I in the midst of them, (Matthew 18:19-20)... 30 How could one pursue a thousand, and two put ten thousand to flight, if his Rock had not sold them, and the Lord had not delivered them up? (Deuteronomy 32:30; 31; 33). Five of you will pursue a hundred, and a hundred of you will pursue ten thousand, and your enemies will fall by the sword before you, (Leviticus 26:8). When the three hundred trumpets sounded, the LORD set the sword against one another throughout the camp; and the army fled to Beth-site, in the direction of Zererah, to the shore of Abel-mehola, near Tabat..." (Judges 7:22-23).

Samuel was prepared by Eli the high priest; "Eli (Ely) in Hebrew means "Exalt Yahweh" who is a biblical personage, High Priest and Judge of Israel, from the family of Ithamar, of the Tribe of Levi. He was the successor of Samson, and predecessor and mentor of the prophet Samuel." Samuel was trained in the priesthood, also from an early age God taught him to recognize his voice. Samuel was prepared to discern between the voice of God and the voice of man.

Jesus prepared for His death, being with the disciples He taught them about His death and resurrection.

3. Execute: Putting the plan into action, applying combat power to complete the mission. The army is managed in concepts of operations, as if it were the police forces, their operation is to control, remove, destroy, remove, and dismantle, stop the crimes that they already know exist. Unified operations is the guide of how to conduct operations, it is similar to offense executions, defenses, stability.

Unified Earth Operations has four rules of unification and control: Change operations from earthly environment, prevent conflict, prevail on a long earthly scale during combat, and consolidate your gains.

The mission of the commander here earthly is to exercise authority and direction properly by placing his commanders assigning and linking forces and powers to complete the mission. The commander mission assigns, controls, empowers, subordinates decisions that are made and decentralizes executes appropriately according to its mission. The mission is based on the way of seeing war that is inherently chaotic uncertain. Many plans change quickly, if a person knows everything properly what to do.

That is why during execution it can change quickly, The commander mission empowers leaders, it does not only make the decisions, but acts according to opportunities and counter-threat. The mission command is competent, shares understanding of the mission, has a mutual trust and mission order. The commander has vision, visualizes, describes, and directs.

You and I are the ones who have to reign here on earth, kings have possessions, they command, they collaborate with the commander's plan, the plan is executed, but we have forgotten something very important and that is evaluation, your duty is to evaluate everything that happens here on earth, including governments, dethroning all principality in global unity with the other churches, Because you believe the enemy attacks unity, because he knows that unity is a powerful tool to destroy him.

The massive operations of earthly and spiritual control is the most important thing here now, when you as a local or regional general, take control of your territorial locality, the demons do not have access to your region, because there is a group of pastors, evangelists, missionaries, teachers, prophets, taking total control and manifesting in a totalitarian movement in the celestial regions of evil, Remember that everything that happens here on earth is because the church is influencing and taking control, if the situation is bad, it is because the church is not governing, and is busy with other things that are not all control. That is why it is important to have eyes on the governmental, educational, judicial elections, all those that are here on earth.

9 But you are a chosen race, a royal priesthood, a holy nation, a people for God's own sake, that you may proclaim the powers of him who called you out of darkness into his marvelous light." (1 Peter 2:9).

6 And he made us kings and priests to God his Father; to him be glory and empire forever and ever. Amen," (Revelation 1:6).

"You are a chosen race, a royal priesthood, a holy nation, a people for special possession, to declare in public the excellencies of him who called you out of darkness into his marvelous light."

If you can see, the Father has already given us the mission, the mission is not only to take the gospel to all nations, as it says in the book of Matthew, but that we are "kings" so it says to rule, institute and tear down every argument that rises in the center of the kingdom of Christ. The most powerful commander who ever lived is Jesus, he told the Sadducees, the law, and all the hypocrites, that his kingdom is over everything and every principality.

And the most beautiful thing is that the church gave it to him. Get rid of the local mentality, because you will be with the mind of a chick and not an eagle. Jesus made known to them by speaking with the word who He was; he spoke with authority not like the Pharisees, or teachers of the law, you have to speak with authority, and move in the power of the Holy Spirit, the ministries are here on earth to work together, as the word says, that's why you should see prophets in all the churches, not just the pastor, but that the gift of prophecies is active, so that when you want to put a Satanist or sorcerer to lead the praises, that prophet that's already there apart from the pastor, can speak for God and expose the enemy.

Every pastor should not be afraid, nor should he criticize the five ministries of the Father. That is why God sent them to work together as a body in which the head is not the shepherd but Christ. Advise the church to enter a Bible college, educate the people to operate in their calling, in the gifts. If you are afraid of being divided by the church, then you are not prepared to lead, in all ministries and affairs of God the flesh will always oppose God. That's why when a pastor is led by the Holy Spirit, when something comes from the sample, and gives him wisdom how to deal with every ministry that is within the church. God showed Pharaohs, kings in the Old Testament of what was going to happen on earth and his kingdom, don't you think God is going to show you what is coming for the church as well? Yes, he will!

But the problem is that you don't want a "Joseph" or an "Elijah" or a Deborah to exercise her gift in your church (i.e., Christ's church). Who are you to stop the things of God and manipulate the gifts within the kingdom of Christ? Every person who enters the church of Christ has a purpose and a calling from God, let the Holy Spirit minister, exhort, teach, prepare and let the kingdom of Christ continue to grow here on earth and not use the pulpit to kill the soldiers of the kingdom of God. Everything that comes out of our mouth will one day be judged.

36 And I say to you, every vain word that men speak, they will give an account of it in the day of judgment" (Matthew 12:36).

Do you think I'm going to lose my salvation because I spoke ill of someone and didn't ask for forgiveness? Bend the flesh right now, and call that brother or that brother or shepherd, sheep, minister and ask him or her to forgive you, for speaking ill of him or her, for using the pulpit in your defense.

We have to change the way of thinking that satan has been filling our heads for many years. If someone says he is a prophet at once we judge him and start preaching about false prophets, if we see an evangelist, all at once, we expel him from the churches or seat him, if we hear about a testimony of prostitutes, we preach about it in the pulpit until the poor sister (or) leaves the church, while we drag the dirty laundry of the brothers from the pulpit.

If we find out that someone fell into sin, we make them feel worse than they did or that they walked through the doors. Many don't come into your church because every time you look at them, they are reminded of how they fell into sin. And enough of us being instruments of stumbling and of satan, accusing the brethren of the churches. Lift, do not overthrow the soldiers of Christ, exhort, do not criticize.

4. Evaluation: Proceeds and guides other activities of the operational process; and concludes each operation or phase as if it were a new operation. Evaluate during the preparation, if the situation can change. For example, if I do a campaign and it rains where I can do it the most, what do I need if something else happens, in that case, what do I do or the church? Retains information to understand and develop the execution of the plan. It's one of the parts that many don't get to break down when they do something for God.

In spiritual warfare, an evaluation is made of why, how to be more effective next time, when they come out of a campaign, which is what to do, many say that the devil is going to attack! And others wait for the devil's bombs because they won souls. I call that having faith in satan, that he's going to counter and attack before you haven't even begun what God has told you to do and you already mention it, what powerful faith in the devil.

In the evaluation, we can put it in the perspective that the Father has left us the Holy Spirit to guide us, to direct us, we have more brothers and sisters that we can call in case of an emergency. Jehovah put Moses, but he also put Aaron, and his own father-in-law so that in difficult times they would be there with him. The most important thing about this step is that our and only sacrifice of the cross was Jesus, there was no other that could take His place, so when He cried out to the Father to...

> *39 And he went a little farther and fell on his face, praying, saying, "My Father, if it be possible, let this cup pass from me; but not as I will, but as you will" (Matthew 36:29).*

The Father was silent, because Jesus was and was the only perfect plan for salvation and redemption, the remission of sins of the world.

The enemy for our adversary needs a body to be able to be more effective in the physical world, but we are already spirit, and we can pass into the spiritual world, but not only can we pass into the spiritual world, but when we pass into the spiritual world, it is in the greatest of the great that is the Holy Spirit within us, that is, those who have been washed with the blood of the lamb and their name are written in the book of life. The spiritual world is more real than the physical world.

That is why a person who says he is a child of God cannot operate only in the physical world effectively, but has to constantly enter the spiritual world, whether it is the second heaven and the third heaven. We are in the second heaven through prayer and intercession, so that the works of satan are not manifested here on earth, so that a man of God and a woman of God cannot stain their clothes with earthly things, that is, have a double life before God, handle themselves by the bony flesh; "Do not make room for the flesh or its conversations to destroy others with your tongue." When you do that, you lose your place of war and you have to re-enter, this time to the third heaven, so that the blood of Christ will cleanse you from all sin. As my son Oniel told me; "The only way to win over the enemy is to know his plan and his intentions." obviously after the Cross and the victory through Jesus Christ.

About The Author

Prophet and Evangelist Elizabeth Walcott is a multifaceted woman who plays roles as a mother, daughter, and sister, as well as being the CEO of Jesus for the Nations (JFTNEnterprises.com) ministry. She is also the announcer and owner of local FM radio 105.5 JFTN-JPLN Inc. in Moline, IL. She conducts conferences and missions globally. She has been called by God to preach and teach within the five ministries, and to equip others and be part of God's authentic prophetic voice.

References

Bermúdez, Á. (2018, April 25). *The brutal and almost forgotten "era of lynchings" of blacks in the United States.* BBC News Mundo.

Michael Jordan [my Father]. (n.d.). In *NBAManiacs*. Retrieved June 24, 2025, from https://www.nbamaniacs.com/noticias/otra-nba/michael-jordan-su-vida-despues-de-retirarse-como-jugador-profesional-de-baloncesto/#:~:text=Despu%C3%A9s%20de%20su%20carrera%20como,y%20a%20favor%20de%20la%20igualmy%20Father

U.S. Department of the Army. (2019). *The operations process* (ADP 5-0). https://irp.fas.org/doddir/army/adp5_0.pdf

Wolf, N. (n.d.). (COVID) and adversity [Personal communication].

www.ingramcontent.com/pod-product-compliance
Lightning Source LLC
Chambersburg PA
CBHW070059080526
44586CB00013B/1124